ANALYTICS
AT WORK

ANALYTICS AT WORK

Smarter Decisions, Better Results

THOMAS H. DAVENPORT
JEANNE G. HARRIS
ROBERT MORISON

HARVARD BUSINESS PRESS
BOSTON, MASSACHUSETTS

14 13 12 11 10   5 4 3 2

Library of Congress Cataloging-in-Publication Data

Davenport, Thomas H., 1954–
    Analytics at work : smarter decisions, better results / Thomas H. Davenport, Jeanne G. Harris, Robert Morison.
        p. cm.
    ISBN 978-1-4221-7769-3 (hardcover : alk. paper)   1. Business intelligence.
2. Decision making.   I. Harris, Jeanne G.   II. Morison, Robert.   III. Title.
    HD38.7.D378 2010
    658.4'013—dc22

                                                    2009032263

The paper used in this publication meets the requirements of the American National Standard for Permanence of Paper for Publications and Documents in Libraries and Archives Z39.48-1992.

Contents

PART TWO

Staying Analytical

Preface

As researchers and writers on business and management, we've thrown a fair number of ideas against the wall. We think they're all great, of course, but it's always difficult to know in advance whether a particular one will stick.

Somewhat to our surprise, the topic of "competing on analytics" stuck. We tapped into a global secular trend toward more data, more computerized analysis of it, and more orientation to fact-based decision making. Each of these trends had been slowly creeping up over time, and just about the time we started publishing in the area, they exploded. We'd attribute this timing to extreme perspicacity except for the fact that many other trends happened largely without our noticing.

So when Tom wrote an article in the *Harvard Business Review* called "Competing on Analytics," and Jeanne and Tom wrote the book by the same name, we immediately saw a lot of demand for speaking and consulting on the subject. In the course of that work we talked with hundreds of managers and analytical professionals in countries all across the globe (except North Korea—we're sure there are analysts there, but we haven't met any). Jeanne also worked with Accenture and its clients to mobilize and coordinate that firm's multiple analytical consulting groups. Tom and Bob led a multicompany research program with nGenera that addressed a variety of topics in the business use of analytics. We decided we should write down what we learned—hence this book.

We all saw a need for more structure around the topic of how to build analytical capabilities. *Competing on Analytics* was about the earliest and most aggressive adopters of analytics, but many other companies and organizations just wanted to know how analytical they were already, and how to become more so over time. They wanted frameworks, assessment tools, examples, and further insights—so we've tried to provide some of each in this book.

This is more of a "how-to" book than its predecessor, but we've tried to avoid the extremes of that genre. We do have a five-part model, and because we want readers to be able to remember it, we've structured it as a catchy little acronym. We continue with the five-stage model for analytical maturity (God has decreed that all maturity models have five stages) that we introduced in the previous book. However, we've resisted saying in exactly what order, or by whom, each step should be taken. There's no fixed methodology here—just some pragmatic suggestions for how to proceed and some frameworks for measuring your progress. It's more a compass than a detailed map.

The first part of the book is a little more framework focused than the second. It addresses the five-letter framework (DELTA) that we've been talking about and applying to companies over the last couple of years. The first part is also more oriented to current practice. Part two opens things up a bit to address some of the capabilities that analytically oriented organizations will need in the future. Some firms are actually addressing those capabilities today.

Acknowledgments

We're collectively grateful for all of the companies that shared their analytical successes and frustrations with us. Some of the companies and managers in the Business Analytics Concours research program were particularly helpful and generous with their time, including David Fogarty at GE Money, Gary Greenwald and Marcia Tal at Citi, Lisa Tourville at Humana, and Pat Steele at Delta Dental of California. We are also grateful to the analytical leaders and analysts we profiled, including Jim and Chris McCann of 1-800-Flowers.com, Tom Anderson of Integrity Interactive, Shannon Antorcha of Carnival Cruise Lines, Greg Poole of Talbots, Joe Megibow of Expedia.com, Steven Udvarhelyi of Independence Blue Cross, Daryl Wansink of Blue Cross and Blue Shield of North Carolina, David Scamehorn of Advance Auto Parts, Tony Branda of RBS, and Marc Gordon and Byrne Doyle of Best Buy.

Several analytics vendors have also been helpful in sponsoring research and events around this topic. SAS has been particularly helpful, and its people particularly pleasant to work with. In particular, we'd like to thank Jim Goodnight, Jim Davis, Scott van Valkenburg, Mike Bright, Michael Coppotelli, Anne Milley, Gaurav Verma, Monet Meek, Ken Bland, Margo Stutesman, and Annette Green.

Other vendor firms that have supported our work include FICO, IBM/Cognos/SPSS, Informatica, InforSense, Intel, Microsoft, Oracle, SAP, Teradata, and Tibco Spotfire. Mike Thompson and Wanda Shive of Waterstone Analytics have been very helpful in sharing their ideas and experiences. Thanks to the companies and the particular individuals involved.

We had four "anonymous" reviewers of the manuscript of this book, but three identified themselves: Ken Demma, Mark McDonald, and Anne Milley. Every single comment they made was helpful, and we've tried to incorporate them all.

Jim Wilson, a great writer and editor, took one last pass at the manuscript in its last month of editing to iron out the wrinkles. We think he did a wonderful job.

At Harvard Business Press, Melinda Merino was—not surprisingly, since we've worked with her before—appropriately encouraging and constructively critical at all the right times. Thanks also to David Goehring for early insights, and to Erin Brown for marketing and PR help.

In terms of individual thanks, Tom sends a grateful nod to his wife Jodi and his sons Hayes and Chase for their love and support. Hayes, a *Harvard Lampoon* alumnus, suggested several mildly humorous additions to the text as well. Tony Paulson suggested some great examples, and Dwight Gertz provided wise counsel about decision making. Tom dedicates his third of the book to Ann and Lawson Hamilton. He will tell them which pages to read later.

Jeanne thanks Accenture's leadership for sharing their enthusiastic support and encouragement along the way. Particular thanks go to Bob Thomas, executive director of the Accenture Institute for High Performance; Accenture CEO Bill Green; Mark Foster, Group Chief Executive of Management Consulting and Global Markets; Dave Rich, Global Managing Director of Analytics and Customer Relationship Management; Royce Bell, CEO of Accenture Information Management Services; and Mark Spelman, Global Managing Director of Strategy, for their consistent support and always-incisive insights. She is grateful to the many senior executives at Accenture who generously shared their candid feedback, real-world experience, and expertise, especially Glenn Gutwillig, Michael Bova, Pierre Puts, George Marcotte, and Brian McCarthy. A special thank-you to friends and colleagues at the Accenture Institute for High Performance for their generous contributions to the analytics research, in particular Allan Alter, Elizabeth Craig, Henry Egan, and Karen Smith.

Jeanne also thanks her husband, Carl, and daughter, Lauren (the real analytical talent in her family), for their patience, love, and inspiration. Thanks also to her sister Susie and to Shawn Nepo for being her biggest fans. Jeanne dedicates her share of this book to Rhoda Harris, for her love, wit, and wisdom, including "Rhoda's more so" principle, which have profoundly enriched her life.

Bob would like to thank members of the research team and other colleagues at The Concours Group and nGenera Corporation who contributed to the Business Analytics Concours research program: Tim Bevins, Jen Bigora, Frank Capek, Laura Carrillo, George Danner, Maira Galins, Mark Martin, Chris O'Leary, and Mark Rennella. Special thanks to Espen Andersen of the Norwegian School of Management and to Ron Christman for his steadfast support of our research and development of better management techniques.

On the personal front, Bob is grateful for the love and support of his wife, Lynne Barrett, and their son, James Barrett-Morison, both superb analysts in their own right.

ANALYTICS
AT WORK

What It Means to Put
Analytics to Work

If we want to make better decisions and take the right actions, we have to use analytics. Putting analytics to work is about improving performance in key business domains using data and analysis. For too long, managers have relied on their intuition or their "golden gut" to make decisions. For too long, important calls have been based not on data, but on the experience and unaided judgment of the decision maker. Our research suggests that 40 percent of major decisions are based not on facts, but on the manager's gut.[1]

Sometimes intuitive and experience-based decisions work out well, but often they either go astray or end in disaster: executives pursue mergers and acquisitions to palliate their egos, neglecting the sober considerations that create real value; banks make credit and risk decisions based on unexamined assumptions about always-rising asset values; governments rely on sparse intelligence before deciding whether to wage war. Such are the most extreme cases of ill-informed decision making.

In other cases, nonanalytical decisions don't lead to tragedy, but they do leave money on the table: businesses price products and services based on their hunches about what the market will bear, not on actual data detailing what consumers have been willing to pay under similar circumstances in the past; managers hire people based on intuition, not on an analysis of the skills and personality traits that predict an employee's high performance; supply chain managers maintain a comfortable level of inventory, rather than a data-determined optimal level; baseball scouts zoom in on players who "look the part," not on those with the skills that—according to analytics—win games.

Socrates said, "The unexamined life isn't worth living." We'd argue that "the unexamined decision isn't worth making."

Consider this firsthand report from an executive with a software company. When asked about a recent sales seminar put on by the firm, he replied: "It went fine. We had attendees from 110 companies who received a keynote presentation designed to instill confidence in our company's future and to encourage cross-selling, and all twelve technical sessions were well received."

That would be enough for many companies. "I guess no decision needs to be made other than to continue holding these seminars at a pace of twelve per quarter around the country," he reflected. But after further thought, he voiced some disquieting questions about what the sales seminar did not reveal:

- How many attendees were existing customers and how many were prospects?

- Were there attendees from every customer within the geographic area?

- Were there attendees from every prospect in the geographic area?

- Which attendees were high-growth prospects?

- How many attendees also attended the company's annual conference?

His company simply didn't know the answers to these questions. It had never bothered to gather and analyze the data. The executive considers his company to be more analytical than most, but, at least with regard to these seminars, it has a long way to go. As this anecdote suggests, even relatively smart and sophisticated companies are missing opportunities to put analytics to work and thereby profit from better decisions.

Companies that continue to manage on autopilot—by having sales seminars because that's what's always been done, for example—are not competing as effectively as they could be. In this book, we'll provide you with a set of tools to make your organization more analytical. We'll demonstrate that becoming more analytical is not solely the responsibility of a manager: it's an essential concern for the entire organization.

What's the payoff for putting analytics to work in your organization? There are many, as shown in "Some Benefits of Being Analytical." We believe it's no accident that the companies we cite as outstanding analytical competitors are often also outstanding performers. Analytics aren't the only way an organization can succeed, but in most industries there are excellent illustrations that the analytical path is a viable route to success.

Some Benefits of Being Analytical

- Help manage and steer the business in turbulent times. Analytics give managers tools to understand the dynamics of their business, including how economic and marketplace shifts influence business performance.

- Know what's really working. Rigorous analytical testing can establish whether your intervention is causing desired changes in your business, or whether it's simply the result of random statistical fluctuations.

- Leverage previous investments in IT and information to get more insight, faster execution, and more business value in many business processes.

- Cut costs and improve efficiency. Optimization techniques can minimize asset requirements and predictive models can anticipate market shifts and enable companies to move quickly to slash costs and eliminate waste.

- Manage risk. Greater regulatory oversight will require more precise metrics and risk management models.

- Anticipate changes in market conditions. You can detect patterns in the vast amount of customer and market data coming your way.

- Have a basis for improving decisions over time. If you are using clear logic and explicit supporting data to make a decision, you or someone else can examine the decision process more easily and try to improve it.

What Do We Mean by "Analytical"?

By analytical we mean the use of analysis, data, and systematic reasoning to make decisions. What kind of analysis? What kind of data? What kind of reasoning? There are no hard-and-fast answers; we contend that almost any analytical process can be good if provided in a serious, systematic fashion.

Many approaches to analysis are fair game, from the latest optimization techniques to tried-and-true versions of root-cause analysis. Perhaps the most common is statistical analysis, in which data are used to make inferences about a population from a sample. Variations of statistical analysis can be used for a huge variety of decisions—from knowing whether something that happened in the past was a result of your intervention, to predicting what may happen in the future. Statistical analysis can be powerful, but it's often complex, and sometimes employs untenable assumptions about the data and the business environment.

When done correctly, statistical analyses can be both simple and valuable. You may remember from your college statistics course that "measures of central tendency"—means, medians, and modes (everybody always forgets what a mode is; it's simply the category with the highest frequency)—are useful ways to express what's going on in data. Sometimes analysis simply means a visual exploration of data in graphic form. You can look at a series of points on a two-dimensional graph, for example, and notice a pattern or relationship. Are there outliers in a pattern that require explanation? Are some values out of range? Visual analysis helps us to "stay close to the data" using "exploratory data analysis," an approach that the great statistician John Tukey made respectable and Edward Tufte further popularized by helping people create clear visual representations of their data.[2]

The key is to always be thinking about how to become *more* analytical and fact based in your decision making and to use the appropriate level of analysis for the decision at hand—and when analyses and decisions are working well, not to rest on your laurels, lest you get stuck in a decision-making rut and be unable to adapt quickly when conditions change.

Some areas of business, like environmental sustainability, haven't historically used data or analysis, so you could become more analytical by creating simple metrics of key activities (for example, a carbon footprint), reporting them on a regular basis, and acting on the patterns that

emerge. This initial step would accomplish a lot—but getting an organization to agree upon metrics in a new area is no easy task.

In other areas, such as customer behavior, you may have so much detailed data available—from a loyalty card program, say, or a Web site—
that making good decisions about how to treat customers requires
sophisticated analytics, including detailed segmentation, scoring customers based on their propensity to exhibit certain behaviors, and next-
best-offer analysis for what customers should buy next. Producing a
mere report would be seriously underachieving in this data-rich domain.

Of course, some forms of analysis don't require quantitative data.
For example, in the fields of corporate anthropology and ethnography,
marketers conduct analysis by systematically observing customers
while they use products or shop in stores. As Yogi Berra noted, "You can
observe a lot just by watching." The most rigorous marketers employ
video and systematic behavior coding to ensure that all recorded behaviors can be analyzed later in detail. Ethnography can help companies
identify problems that customers have with their products and services.
Data gained through observation can also shed light on a statistical association. We may know that men with young families purchase both
beer and diapers in the grocery store, but only systematic observation
can reveal which they buy first, and whether it makes sense to shelve
them in close proximity or at opposite ends of the store.

The most analytical firms and managers employ a combination of
techniques, both quantitative and qualitative. eBay, for example, under-
takes extensive and varied analyses by performing randomized tests of
Web page variations before making any change to the Web site or the
business model. With more than a billion page views per day, eBay can
run thousands of such experiments, many concurrently. To make sense
of all these tests, eBay built its own application, called the eBay Experimentation Platform, to lead testers through the process and to keep
track of what's being tested at what times on what pages. Of course, you
may not feel that you can undertake the kinds of complex and detailed
testing and analyses that eBay, blessed with a massive amount of data
(all those mouse clicks), can support.

But in addition to online testing, eBay considers changes to its Web
site using a variety of analytical approaches: the company conducts extensive, face-to-face testing with its customers, including lab studies,
home visits, participatory design sessions, focus groups, and iterative
trade-off analysis. eBay also conducts quantitative visual design research

and eye-tracking studies, and diary studies to see how users feel about potential changes. The company will make no significant changes to its site without these analyses. This analytical orientation is not the only reason eBay is successful, but it's clearly one factor, with 113 million items for sale in over fifty thousand categories at any given time.

It's not our goal in this book to provide you with a list of all possible analytical tools, but rather to persuade you that putting analytics to work can help your managers and employees make better decisions, and help your organization perform better. Analytics aren't just a way of looking at a particular problem, but rather an organizational capability that can be measured and improved. It is our goal to describe the primary components of that capability and the best ways to strengthen them. Think of this book as therapy for your organization's analytical brain.

What Kinds of Questions Can Analytics Answer?

Every organization needs to answer some fundamental questions about its business. Taking an analytical approach begins with anticipating how information will be used to address common questions (see figure 1-1). These questions are organized across two dimensions:

- *Time frame.* Are we looking at the past, present, or future?

- *Innovation.* Are we working with known information or gaining new insight?

The matrix in figure 1-1 identifies the six key questions that data and analytics can address in organizations. The first set of challenges is using information more effectively. The "past" information cell is the realm of traditional business reporting, rather than analytics. By applying rules of thumb, you can generate alerts about the present—what's happening right now (like whenever an activity strays outside of its normal performance pattern). Using simple extrapolation of past patterns creates information about the future, such as forecasts. All of these questions are useful to answer, but they don't tell you why something happens or how likely it is to recur.

The second set of questions requires different tools to dig deeper and produce new insights. Insight into the past is gained by statistical modeling activities, which explain how and why things happened. Insight into the present takes the form of recommendations about what to do

FIGURE 1-1

Key questions addressed by analytics

	Past	Present	Future
Information	What happened? (Reporting)	What is happening now? (Alerts)	What will happen? (Extrapolation)
Insight	How and why did it happen? (Modeling, experimental design)	What's the next best action? (Recommendation)	What's the best/worst that can happen? (Prediction, optimization, simulation)

right now—for example, what additional product offering might interest a customer. Insight into the future comes from prediction, optimization, and simulation techniques to create the best possible future results.

Together these questions encompass much of what an organization needs to know about itself. The matrix can also be used to challenge existing uses of information. You may find, for example, that many of your "business intelligence" activities are in the top row. Moving from purely information-oriented questions to those involving insights is likely to give you a much better understanding of the dynamics of your business operations.

Analytics for the Rest of Us

In our previous book, *Competing on Analytics*, we described companies that build their entire strategies around their analytical capabilities. We were gratified by the success of a book on such a nerdy topic, and we certainly still believe that analytical competition is a viable strategic choice for companies in almost every industry.

However, as we talked about the book to readers and conference attendees around the world, we found that we'd missed a big audience. Many of our readers worked in companies that didn't want to become analytical competitors, but rather wanted to move their organizations toward greater analytical maturity. They believed that making decisions on facts and analytics was beneficial, but they didn't necessarily want to build their companies and value propositions around doing so. Although they politely listened to our speeches and praised our book, we could see that they were really in the market for some slightly different ideas.

While we suspect this book will be of great interest to analytical competitors, it speaks more directly to a broader base of organizations: those aiming to become more analytical. If you think that your organization ought to make more decisions based on facts (not unaided intuition or prejudice), or if you want to unleash the potential buried in your company's data, this book will help you. We still urge companies, over time, to move toward a mentality and strategy of competing on analytics—we think that's where the greatest benefits lie. But those who seek a more incremental approach can still be more analytical, even if primarily competing on other factors, such as product innovation, customer relationships, operational excellence, and so forth.

In this book we occasionally refer to analytical competitors, such as Harrah's Entertainment, Capital One, and Progressive Insurance, because they are great repositories of leading analytical practices. But most of the companies we describe in this book are not aggressive analytical competitors—they've just figured out how to make more analytical decisions and have profited from them.

Why It's Time to Put Analytics to Work

Most companies today have massive amounts of data at their disposal. The data may come from transaction-oriented applications such as ERP (enterprise resource planning) systems from software vendors such as SAP and Oracle, scanner data in retail environments, customer loyalty programs, financial transactions, or clickstream data from customer Web activity. But what do they do with all this information? Not nearly enough.

Managers we interviewed at a retail grocery chain confessed to this deficiency when we asked them what they did with their data. One manager said, "Well, we sell it. In fact, we make more money selling data to retail data syndication firms than we do selling meat." We dutifully said that result was impressive, but the firm's managers also admitted to a less impressive fact—that they later buy back their own data, mixed with that of local competitors.

"What else do you do with it?" we asked.

"We store it on disk," they told us. "Then we put it on tape. Then we store it under a mountain so that it's safe from nuclear attack."

"But what do you actually do with it to manage your business?" we persisted.

"Not much," they confessed. "That's why we wanted to talk with you."

Companies, governments, and nonprofits, in sophisticated economies and developing nations alike, stumble over the same ineffective strategies as this retailer. They collect and store a lot of data, but they don't use it effectively. They have information and they make decisions, but they don't analyze the information to inform their decision making.

Of course, companies won't become analytical all at once. Instead, they will do so one decision at a time. They'll look at individual decisions and say, "We can do better." Then they'll apply fact-based and quantitative analysis to make that decision more accurately, more consistently, and with an eye toward the future, rather than just reporting on the past. When they realize how much better they make that one decision, they'll move on to others. To some extent, this creeping improvement of decisions is inevitable as our society becomes more computerized, data-rich, and analytical. However, those who move forward with intent and urgency have an edge over those who simply evolve.

Where Do Analytics Apply?

Analytics can help to transform just about any part of your business or organization. Many organizations start where they make their money—in customer relationships. They use analytics to segment their customers and identify their best ones. They analyze data to understand customer behaviors, predict their customers' wants and needs, and offer fitting products and promotions. They ensure that the money and resources devoted to marketing focus on the most effective campaigns and channels. They price products for maximum profitability at levels that they know their customers will pay. Finally, they identify the customers at greatest risk of attrition, and intervene to try to keep them.

Supply chain and operations is also an area where analytics are commonly put to work. The most effective supply chain organizations optimize inventory levels and delivery routes, for example. They also segment their inventory items by cost and velocity, build key facilities in the best locations, and ensure that the right products are available in the right quantities. If they're in service businesses, they measure and fine-tune service operations.

Human resources, a traditionally intuitive domain, increasingly uses analytics in hiring and employee retention. Just as sports teams analyze data to pick and keep the best players, firms are using analytical criteria to select valuable employees and identify those who are most likely to depart. They're also identifying which operational employees should work at which times to maximize sales and profits.

Not surprisingly, analytics can also be applied to the most numerical of business areas: finance and accounting. Instead of just putting financial and nonfinancial metrics on scorecards, leading firms are using analytics to determine which factors truly drive financial performance. In this era of instability, financial and other firms are using analytics to monitor and reduce risk. And recent problems in the investment industry notwithstanding, no one really believes that the serious business of investment can proceed without analytics. In banking and insurance, the use of analytics to issue credit and underwrite insurance policies grows ever more common and sophisticated.

We have little doubt that the use of analytics will continue to grow—in businesses, nonprofits, and governments—in part because the volume and variety of available data will continue to grow. As more processes are automated and instrumented with sensors, the only way to control them efficiently is to analyze the vast volumes of data they produce. Today, smart grids use analytics to optimize and reduce energy usage for sustainability. Someday, we may live on a "smart planet," with the ability to monitor and analyze all aspects of the environment. It's already an analytical world, and it will only become more so.

When Are Analytics Not Practical?

We feel strongly that most organizations can benefit from a more analytical approach. However, there are some times when being analytical just doesn't fit the situation. These include the following:

When There's No Time. Some decisions must be made before data can be gathered systematically. One of the best examples is the decision Gary Klein addresses in his book *Sources of Power*.[3] When a firefighter is in a burning building, trying to decide whether the floor is about to collapse, he has to "gather data" rapidly by observing his surroundings. He's unlikely to perform a logistic regression analysis.

When There's No Precedent. If something has never been done before, it's hard to get data about it. The obvious analytical response in such a situation is to perform a small-scale randomized test on the idea and see if it works. But sometimes testing isn't possible, either. Mike Linton, formerly the chief marketing officer for Best Buy, says that it's not always possible to use analytics before making marketing decisions: "You have to mix the 'ready/aim/fire' analytical decision making with the 'ready/fire/aim' approaches sometimes. For example, we tied a new Paul McCartney CD we were selling exclusively with promotion of his concert tour. That had never been done before, to our knowledge, and we couldn't test it. You use all the decision tools at your disposal, but sometimes you have to go with intuition."[4] It is worth noting, though, that Best Buy defines beforehand how it will evaluate the success and impact of such experiments, thus creating new insights and building a platform for making fact-based decisions the next time.

When History Is Misleading. Even when ample precedents exist, as the fine print on the stockbroker ads warns, "past performance is not necessarily indicative of future results." Improbable, unpredictable events, called "black swans" by Nassim Nicholas Taleb, are immune to analysis.[5] Though Taleb unwisely discounts all statistical analysis because of these anomalies, statistical analysis is very useful most of the time. Rather than abandoning statistics altogether, companies should try to identify those unusual times when the past is not a good guide to the present.

When the Decision Maker Has Considerable Experience. Sometimes a decision maker has made a particular decision often enough to have internalized the process of gathering and analyzing data. If you're an experienced home appraiser, for example, you can approximate what a home is worth without feeding data into an algorithm.

When the Variables Can't Be Measured. Some decisions are difficult to make analytically because the key variables in the analysis are hard to measure with rigor. For example, while the process of finding a romantic partner or spouse has been the subject of considerable quantitative analysis (as employed by firms such as eHarmony), we're not strong believers in the power of analytics to help you choose a mate. Analytics can be a start, but cannot replace intuitive judgments in such domains; you may want to meet your "match" in person before buying a ring!

Even though they're not always feasible, analytics are valuable enough that they should be the first, rather than the last, resort in making decisions. In many intuitive organizations, analytics are merely a rationalization, wherein data is selected to support a decision that's already been made. As the Scottish writer Andrew Lang commented, "Statistics are often used as a drunken man uses a lamppost—for support rather than illumination." Intuition, too often the default tool of decision makers, should be employed only when there is no alternative. Even in the circumstances listed above, in which intuition is appropriate, it's worthwhile to track the intuition applied, the decisions made, and the results. Over time, such recordkeeping can turn intuition into rules of thumb and even algorithms.

When Analytical Decisions Need Scrutiny

We are inevitably headed to a more analytical future; you can't put all the data genies back in their server bottles. But if we are going to use analytics, we have to do it well. The same process and logic errors that cause people to err without analytics can creep into analytical decisions. *Analytics at Work* is a guidebook for smart people who want to learn how to avoid the pitfalls shown in "Typical Decision-Making Errors."

As "Typical Decision-Making Errors" demonstrates, even companies with the best intentions of being analytical can err in many ways if not careful. For example, a Canadian power generation firm, TransAlta, made a spreadsheet error that cost the company $24 million in hedging contracts.[6] NASA famously lost a $125 million Mars Orbiter spacecraft by neglecting to consistently employ the metric system in its analyses. The state of North Carolina based an important decision on a faulty model that incorporated overly positive assumptions about the jobs and sales taxes that new employers in the state would bring. As a result, the state gave out millions of dollars in incentives that may not have been warranted.[7]

North Carolina's misstep demonstrates a typical problem: analytical thinking based on invalid or outdated assumptions. Every quantitative

Typical Decision-Making Errors

Logic Errors

- Not asking the right questions

- Making incorrect assumptions and failing to test them

- Using analytics to justify what you want to do (gaming or rigging the model/data) instead of letting the facts guide you to the right answer

- Failing to take the time to understand all the alternatives or interpret the data correctly

Process Errors

- Making careless mistakes (transposed numbers in a spreadsheet or a mistake in a model)

- Failing to consider analysis and insights in decisions

- Failing to consider alternatives seriously

- Using incorrect or insufficient decision-making criteria

- Gathering data or completing analysis too late to be of any use

- Postponing decisions because you're always dissatisfied with the data and analysis you already have

analysis is based on assumptions. Technical assumptions might include a belief that a sample is randomly selected or that data are normally distributed. Assumptions about the world that a model reflects may encourage the erroneous belief that factors outside the model are held constant, when they actually aren't. Most models assume accuracy only within the range of data gathered, barring the possibility of accurate predictions or explanations outside of the model's specific times, geographies, or types of people. Attempting to judge factors outside of the model's range could cause serious trouble. That was one of the problems in the recent financial crisis (see "Analytics and the 2007–2009 Financial Crisis").

Analytics and the 2007–2009 Financial Crisis

It's clear that the financial services industry has used analytics in the wrong way. The financial industry's subprime crisis in 2007–2009 illustrates many analytical approaches gone wrong. For example, banks used analytics to issue subprime mortgage loans. Many firms continued to make loans even though a close analysis of the data would have suggested that many customers were beginning to default on them.

A series of faulty assumptions compounded the problem: Wall Street "quants" included an excessive number of years of history in their trading models for mortgage-backed securities to make them look less risky;[a] mortgage lending models relied on the assumption that housing prices would continue to rise; and credit default models were based on the assumption of liquidity in credit markets.

It's also clear that risk analytics are not what they should be. AIG became a government-owned firm primarily because of its inability to price and predict credit defaults; Moody's, Standard & Poors, and Fitch were clearly unable to assess the risk of mortgage-backed securities and attach accurate credit ratings to them. The 1987 stock market crash was caused in part by a similar inability to assess the risk of portfolio insurance.

Going forward, financial firms need to radically change their analytical focus. They need to make the assumptions behind the models much more explicit and transparent. They need to incorporate the systematic monitoring of analytical models into their businesses. They—and their regulators—need to be skeptical about the ability to model and manage risk in extraordinary circumstances.

Perhaps most important, financial executives need to learn much more about the models that are running their businesses. In search of outsized returns, they've taken on investment and debt securities that are bundled up in algorithmic combinations that they don't understand. Cowed by this accumulation of daunting numbers, these executives have abdicated responsibility for managing risk. If you're a U.S. citizen, you now own part of several such firms; wouldn't you prefer that the executives running your business understand how it works?

a. Saul Hansell, "How Wall Street Quants Lied to Their Computers," *New York Times* blog, http://bits.blogs.nytimes.com/2008/09/18/how-wall-streets-quants-lied-to-their-computers/.

Not everyone was drawn into poor analytical decisions in the financial services industry. For example, according to an article about Wells Fargo:

> Richard Kovacevich, chairman of Wells Fargo, and his lieutenants deliberately steered clear of the riskiest sorts of subprime mortgages—"stated income" or "low documentation" loans to borrowers with sketchy credit. They stayed out even though it caused them to lose market share in the short term that would have generated big loan fees. "We talked about what others [banks, investment firms and mortgage brokers] were doing," but decided "it's economically unsound" and "doesn't make sense," he says. By making such risky loans to financially stretched borrowers, "you're basically saying, 'Defraud me,' " adds Mr. Kovacevich, whose bank has avoided the huge losses incurred at rivals. Giving that kind of loan "isn't in our DNA."[8]

Maybe it takes an analytical CEO to understand these now-obvious risks. Kovacevich of Wells Fargo is known for his interest in fact-based decision making and quantitative testing. The bank has done pretty well in the current crisis, and was able to pick up a large rival, Wachovia, at a bargain price. Ed Clark, the CEO of Toronto Dominion Bank and a Harvard PhD in economics, also resisted the subprime wave, and insisted that his managers understand the deals they did buy into.[9]

As the financial and investment industries (and for that matter, all industries) become more data oriented and analytical, it is incumbent upon senior executives to master some degree of analytical complexity. Otherwise, they're not going to be able to push back when some trader suggests that they take on inordinate and poorly understood risk, putting their institutions and their customers in great jeopardy.

Combining Art and Science

Analytics will continue to be critical in financial services and all other industries, so the best decision makers will be those who combine the science of quantitative analysis with the art of sound reasoning. Such art comes from experience, conservative judgment, and the savvy to question and push back on assumptions that don't make sense. Art also plays a role in creatively formulating and solving problems—from data collection to modeling to imagining how results can best be deployed and managed.

A good illustration of the art of judgment arose when one of us (Tom) was talking casually with an airline pilot at a social gathering about his work on analytics. The pilot responded, "Oh, yes, we've got lots of that in modern airliners—avionics, lots of computers, 'fly by wire,' and all that. But I still occasionally find it useful to look out the window." A good business executive will take the pilot's advice—certainly pay attention to the computers and analytics that help to run the business, but always look out the window for threats that the analytical models can't predict.

Some firms actively try to balance art and science. Netflix's CEO, Reed Hastings, started the company with a strong scientific orientation, but he tries to ensure that managers and employees don't neglect art in decisions. For example, he sponsored a series of discussions on story-telling to ensure that Netflix employees could express even analytical results in a compelling narrative form.

Netflix's chief content officer, Ted Sarandos, is responsible for choosing films that Netflix will distribute. He confirms the need for art and science: "For a technology company like Netflix, we are the group that is most dependent on art. What we do is probably 70 percent science, 30 percent art. Our buying staff has to have their finger on the pulse of the market to make their decisions. A high box-office performer won't necessarily be a high video performer, and vice versa. The box office is an indicator, as a proxy for awareness, but not for demand."[10]

In a variety of ways, art is already built into analytics. First is the hypothesis, which is really an intuition about what's happening in the data. Hypotheses enter the realm of science when subjected to the requisite testing.

Choosing the business area to support with analytics also requires art. As we describe in chapter 5, creating targets for analytical activity calls for a mixture of intuition, strategy and management frameworks, and experience. To choose the best target, the decision maker must also have a vision of where a company and its industry are headed and what its customers will value in the future. This kind of integrative, big-picture assessment is something that human brains tend to do better than computers.

Art also comes in when smart, experienced humans decide that their analytical models no longer apply. Recognizing the limits of analytics is a key human trait that will not change.

While analytics are not perfect, we prefer them to the shoddy alternatives of bias, prejudice, self-justification, and unaided intuition. Humans often make long lists of excuses not to be analytical, but there's plenty of research showing that data, facts, and analysis are powerful aids to decision making, and that the decisions made on them are better than those made through intuition or gut instinct. Therefore, use analytics. If you can measure and analyze something, do it—but don't forget to incorporate your experience, knowledge, and qualitative insights about the world.

Finally, what makes analytical organizations so interesting, in our view, is the needed combination of human and computational perspectives. Analytical decision making is at the intersection of individual and organizational capabilities. How analytical an organization becomes depends upon the quality of the sum total of decisions across the organization—decisions made by distributed decision makers who may not even talk to each other about the role of analytics in their deliberations. The quality and analytical soundness of those decisions depends on not just the intelligence and experience of the decision makers, but on a host of organizational factors that can be assessed and improved. We'll spend the next ten chapters talking about them.

Part One

The Analytical
DELTA

What does it take to put analytics to work in your business? What capabilities and assets do you need in order to succeed with analytics initiatives? The next five chapters describe the success factors. We group them under the acronym DELTA—the Greek letter (depicted as Δ or δ) that signifies "change" in an equation. Together they can change your business equation:

D for accessible, high-quality *data*

E for an *enterprise orientation*

L for analytical *leadership*

T for strategic *targets*

A for *analysts*

Why are these elements so important? First of all, good *data* is the prerequisite for everything analytical; it is "clean" in terms of accuracy and format. Customer data, for example, has a unique identifier for each customer, and customer names, addresses, and purchase histories are generally accurate. Its meaning and use are commonly understood. When drawn from several sources, it is integrated and consistent. It is accessible in data warehouses, or else easily found, filtered, and formatted on the fly. Perhaps most fundamentally, it represents and measures something new, something important, or something important in a new way. In chapter 2 we detail the essentials of data management for analytics.

Several of the challenges of data management are much easier to meet if the *enterprise* at large "owns" important data—as well as analytical software and talent—and management across the enterprise is motivated to cooperate on analytical initiatives. You might ask, "But we're starting small, with a specific problem in a single business function—why would we need an enterprise perspective?" The short answer is that you won't get far without one, for three reasons:

1. Major analytics applications, those that really improve performance and competitiveness, invariably touch multiple parts of the enterprise.

2. If your applications are cross-functional, it doesn't make sense to manage your key resources—data, analysts, and technology—locally.

3. Without an enterprise perspective, chances are you'll have many small analytical initiatives but few, if any, significant ones.

In chapter 3, we discuss how the definition of "enterprise" varies across organizations and how to manage key analytical resources at an enterprise level.

Organizations that really capitalize on analytics in their business decisions, processes, and customer relationships have a special kind of *leadership*. Their senior managers are not just committed to the success of specific analytical projects; they have a passion for managing by fact. Their long-term goal is not just to apply analytics in useful areas of the business, but to become more analytical in decision-making styles and methods across the enterprise. In chapter 4, we describe the key attributes of analytical leaders and what they do.

Even very analytically inclined leaders are not going to write blank checks to fund analytics generally. What really gets their attention is the potential return of employing analytics where it will make a substantial difference. An analytical *target* may be strong customer loyalty, highly efficient supply chain performance, more precise asset and risk management, or even hiring, motivating, and managing high-quality people. Companies need targets because they cannot be equally analytical about all aspects of their businesses, and analytical talent isn't plentiful enough to cover all bases. In chapter 5 we describe what makes for good targets, and how to evaluate and choose realistic ones.

Analysts have two chief functions: they build and maintain models that help the business hit its analytical targets, and they bring analytics to the organization at large by enabling businesspeople to appreciate and apply them. In chapter 6 we describe the different types of analysts, the methods to assess and improve their capabilities, and the organizational forms that bring out their best. We draw on an extensive survey of analysts that reveals what they want from their jobs and employers.

You need all five elements working together. Lack of any one of the DELTA elements can be a roadblock to success, providing fodder for the naysayers, the "this will never work around here" crowd. A missing element will lead to delay and wasted effort, so if you are better positioned in one element, try to leverage that strength to generate interest in bringing the others along. If some DELTA elements are too far ahead of others, it can lead to frustration, as when leadership sees targets and wants results, but the data or the analysts aren't ready. You can also overspend on getting one element—typically data—ready, and then have it sit dormant because none of the other ingredients are in place.

Thus, to make real progress, you've got to move forward with all five DELTA elements in rough proportion. But organizations have very different starting points, different mixes of capability, and different rates of progress with analytics. To help you sort all this out and to plan and manage your development of analytical capabilities, we developed a five-stage model of progress (which we also described in *Competing on Analytics*):

- *Stage 1: Analytically Impaired.* The organization lacks one or several of the prerequisites for serious analytical work, such as data, analytical skills, or senior management interest.

- *Stage 2: Localized Analytics.* There are pockets of analytical activity within the organization, but they are not coordinated or focused on strategic targets.

- *Stage 3: Analytical Aspirations.* The organization envisions a more analytical future, has established analytical capabilities, and has a few significant initiatives under way, but progress is slow—often because some critical DELTA factor has been too difficult to implement.

- *Stage 4: Analytical Companies.* The organization has the needed human and technological resources, applies analytics regularly, and realizes benefits across the business. But its strategic focus is not grounded in analytics, and it hasn't turned analytics to competitive advantage.

- *Stage 5: Analytical Competitors.* The organization routinely uses analytics as a distinctive business capability. It takes an enterprise-wide approach, has committed and involved leadership, and has achieved large-scale results. It portrays itself both internally and externally as an analytical competitor.

We are not suggesting that becoming an "analytical competitor" is appropriate or necessary for all organizations, but most organizations will at least want to become more analytical, and move up a stage or two. In the next five chapters, we describe how each of the DELTA elements evolves across the stages. Data, for example, moves from poor to usable, to consolidated, to integrated, to innovative. Leadership moves from none to local, to aware, to supportive, to passionate.

For easy reference, in the appendix we combine this model of progress with the DELTA success factors in a table that portrays the conditions at each stage of progress. It can serve as a high-level assessment tool for your analytical capability, a map for locating where you are and where you need to go next.

Use the information and tools in these five chapters (and the appendix) to orient yourself analytically—assess your capabilities, add new capabilities, set realistic goals, get the pieces in place for analytical business initiatives, and proceed with confidence. Getting the pieces in place is especially important if your business is just starting to employ analytics in significant ways. Early success builds momentum for continued success.

2

DATA

The Prerequisite for Everything Analytical

YOU CAN'T BE ANALYTICAL without data, and you can't be really good at analytics without really good data. Now, on to the next chapter!

Well, in case you need more information, the rest of this chapter is about the data environment your organization needs to become more analytical. We'll begin by describing the key components of data management for analytics as employed by the most sophisticated or "stage 5" companies. As we suggest in the introduction to part one, not every organization needs to be at stage 5 for data, but unlike other topics in this book, data management is best addressed by considering how close your organization can come to this ideal. Next we'll discuss how to progress from stage to stage to improve your data and data management for analytics—and even if you're already pretty good, you still need to know about stage 5 data management for analytics.

Here's what you need to know about data, moving from the most fundamental issues onward: structure (what is the nature of the data you have?), uniqueness (how do you exploit data that no one else has?), integration (how do you consolidate it from various sources?), quality (how do you rely on it?), access (how do you get at it?), privacy (how do you guard it?), and governance (how do you pull it all together?). We'll take each topic in turn.

Structure

Companies basically have a choice of three methods of structuring data for analysis: "cubes," arrays, and nonnumeric. If you are tempted to stop reading and tune into ESPN or the Weather Channel, stick with us for a while—the topic is less dry than it sounds. How your data is structured matters because it affects the types of analyses you can do.

Data in transaction systems is generally stored in tables. Tables are very good for processing transactions and for making lists, but less useful for analysis. (One reason: tables rarely contain historical data—three to twelve months at most.) So when data is extracted from a database or transaction system and stored in a warehouse, it frequently is formatted into "cubes." Data cubes are collections of prepackaged multidimensional tables. For example, sales by region by quarter would yield a conventional, three-dimensional cube. However, (unlike the physical world) "data cubes" can have more than three dimensions (though more than four or five can be confusing to carbon-based life forms). Cubes are useful for reporting and "slicing and dicing" data, but less useful for analytical exploration because the variables they contain are limited to what some analyst thought should be in the cube and in the resulting report.

Data arrays consist of structured content, such as numbers in rows and columns (a spreadsheet is a specialized form of array). By storing your data in this format, you can use a particular field or variable for analysis if it is in the database. Arrays may consist of hundreds or even thousands of variables. This format allows for the most flexibility, but may be confusing to nontechnical users who don't understand the structure of the database or the locations and fields of the data within it.

Unstructured, nonnumeric data—the "last frontier" for data analysis—isn't in the formats or content types that databases normally contain. It can take a variety of forms, and companies are increasingly interested in analyzing it. You may hypothesize, for example, that the vocal tone of your customers during service calls is a good predictor of how likely they are to remain customers, so you would want to capture that attribute. Or you may analyze social media—blogs, Web pages, and Web-based ratings and comments—to understand consumer sentiments about your company. In this case, the entire Internet becomes the data warehouse (although you may want to extract and copy some of it for detailed analysis). Firms are also increasingly interested in mining text in internal databases—like warranty reports and customer complaint letters—for customer services issues, "reason fields" (for example, in denying credit), and product descriptions (for example, to reconcile multiple product hierarchies following mergers and acquisitions). There's potential value in unstructured data, but just like mining for gold, you have to sort through a lot of dirt to find what you want. For example, words that you really care about—like *fire*—can have a variety of meanings, so you have to do some semantic analysis to be sure you're getting the meanings you want.

Highly analytical (stage 5) organizations, then, engage in many different projects involving both cubes and arrays. They also tend to use, or at least experiment with, a wider variety of data—not just numbers, but data like images, Web text, and voice analyses.

Uniqueness

How can you tap into and exploit data that no one else has? Inevitably, companies that have the same data will have similar analytics. To get an analytical edge, you must have some unique data. For instance, no one else knows what your customers bought from you—and you can certainly get value from that data. But deciding what information is valuable and going out and getting proprietary data that doesn't exist in your or anybody else's organization is a different matter, and may require creating a new metric.

As Al Parisian, chief information officer and head of strategic planning for Montana State Fund, notes, "You are what you eat with regard to data . . . Just as a seriously health-oriented person must get much more engaged with what they eat, those who are serious about informing fact-based leadership must get very engaged with data."[1] We concur, and conclude that a unique strategy requires unique data. Since stage 5 organizations by definition seek an edge with their analytical capabilities, they need to seek data that other firms don't have or use.

There are several levels of unique data: one is simply to be the first company in your industry to use commercially available data. Progressive Insurance did this in 1996 when it began to use consumers' credit scores as an input to its automobile insurance underwriting. Whether you pay your bills turned out to be a surprisingly good predictor of whether you will crash your car—no one knows exactly why—but it took other firms in the industry at least four years to start using this data (and some still haven't caught on).

It was inevitable that competitors would catch up to Progressive, because anybody can buy a credit score and competitive secrets don't stay secret for long—particularly in the insurance industry, which has to publish underwriting approaches in regulatory filings. Nevertheless, Progressive kept innovating in other areas, as we describe in chapter 9, proving that even if you're using industry-standard data and your competitors have glommed onto the idea, it's still possible to differentiate your company with that data. Capital One, for example, made extensive use of consumer credit scores for extending credit and pricing in its credit card business, but soon most of its competitors followed suit. So it started to fool around with the credit score data, determining through detailed analysis that some low-score applicants might be more likely to pay back their loans than the score would predict. By identifying some data that differentiates customers, it was able to differentiate its own services—even though the initial input was a widely employed data source.

Of course, it's easier to get proprietary advantage when the data is sourced from internal operations or customer relationships. Let's look at some examples of the latter:

- Olive Garden, an Italian restaurant chain owned by Darden Restaurants, uses data on store operations to forecast almost every aspect of its restaurants. The guest forecasting application produces forecasts for staffing and food preparation down to the individual menu item and component. Over the past two years, Darden has reduced unplanned staff hours by more than 40 percent and cut food waste by 10 percent.[2]

- The Nike+ program uses sensors in running shoes to collect data on how far and fast its customers run. The data is uploaded to the runner's iPod, and then to the Nike Web site. Through analysis of this data, Nike has learned that the most popular day for running is Sunday, that wearers of Nike+ shoes tend to work out after 5 p.m., and that many runners set new goals as part of their New Year's resolutions. Nike has also learned that after five uploads, a runner is likely to be hooked on the shoe and the program.[3]

- Best Buy was able to determine through analysis of its Reward-Zone loyalty program member data that its best customers

represented only 7 percent of total customers, but were responsible for 43 percent of its sales. It then segmented its stores to
focus on the needs of these customers in an extensive "customer
centricity" initiative.

- In the United Kingdom, the Royal Shakespeare Company carefully examined ticket sales data that it had accumulated over
seven years to grow its share of wallet of existing customers—
and to identify new audiences. Using audience analytics to look
at names, addresses, shows attended, and prices paid for tickets,
the RSC developed a targeted marketing program that increased
the number of "regulars" by more than 70 percent.[4]

- Consumer packaged goods companies often don't know their
customers, but Coca-Cola has developed a relationship with
(mostly young) customers through the MyCokeRewards.com
Web site, which the company believes has increased its sales
and allowed it to market to consumers as individuals. The site
attracts almost three hundred thousand visitors a day—up
13,000 percent from 2007 to 2008.[5]

- A top ten U.S. bank with over three thousand branches found
it nearly doubled the balance per customer interaction by using
collaboration-based analytic technology when dealing with
customers. First-year profitability per interaction increased
by 75 percent after taking into account the additional value
provided to the customers by the bank. Sales productivity
of front-line bank staff also increased by almost 100 percent
in terms of balances sold per hour.

Of course, data that was once unique and proprietary can become
commoditized too. For example, every airline has a loyalty program, but
these programs all offer similar benefits, and the data from them is not
generally used to create and maintain strong relationships with customers. At one point these programs were great, but now they are simply a me-too capability. There is probably some potential for an airline to
break out from the pack and do something distinctive with its loyalty
data, but most airlines are perhaps too preoccupied with fuel costs and
mergers to seize this opportunity.

Data gold mines can also potentially come from basic company
operations, if the company realizes their value. For example, Cisco

Systems has been maintaining the data (and increasingly voice) networks of its customers for years. Recently, the company realized that it could analyze the data on network configurations to identify which customers were mostly likely to be facing a network failure and would need to upgrade equipment. Cisco can benchmark and analyze a customer's network and all its component products across multiple dimensions— the network's configuration, its use, the position of devices in the network, and so forth. It can predict the network's stability and anticipate pending problems like "toxic combinations" of network equipment. Cisco analysts can also compare a network's likely stability to that of others in the same industry or of similar size. The ability to do such diagnoses differentiates Cisco's services and improves sales of its products.

Many more organizations will, we predict, realize that their operational data is an important asset. Delta Dental of California realized that by analyzing years of claims data, it could begin to understand patterns of behavior among insured customers and the dentists it pays: are a particular dentist's patients developing more problems than others? Are root canals more common in some areas than others? Another health insurer realized that it could identify older insured customers at risk of diabetes from inactivity, and now works to head off the disease through a program called Silver Sneakers Steps (run by Healthways, a disease management company), which uses a pedometer to measure daily steps taken.

A proprietary performance metric can also lead to improved decision making that can differentiate one company from another. Wal-Mart used the ratio of wages to sales at the store level as a new indicator of performance. Marriott created a new revenue management metric called "revenue opportunity" that relates actual revenues to optimal revenues at a particular property. Even if the metric already exists in other industries, if it's not yet used in yours, it can create some value. Harrah's, for example, imported the metric of "same store sales" from the retail industry, and was the first to employ it in the casino business. Harrah's also measured the frequency of employee smiles on the casino floor, because it determined that they were positively associated with customer satisfaction. All that remains for Harrah's, seemingly, is correlating a player's success in craps against the number of times he blows on a pair of dice.

Regardless of the source of proprietary data, any organization that wants to succeed with analytics needs to start identifying some data that it alone possesses. The next decade is going to see an explosion of attempts to analyze proprietary data. Stage 5 companies are doing it today.

Integration

Data integration, which is the aggregation of data from multiple sources inside and outside an organization, is critical for organizations that want to be more analytical. Transactional systems are often "stovepiped," addressing only a particular part of the business, such as order management, human resources, or customer relationship management. Enterprise resource planning (ERP) systems, which cover broad business functionality, are a notable exception. Thanks to these, organizations have come closer to solving a lot of the basic data integration challenges that bedeviled the early years of IT management. But even with an ERP system in place, you will undoubtedly need to consolidate and integrate data from a variety of systems if you want to do analytical work.

For example, you may want to do analysis to find out whether shipping delays affect what your customers buy from you—a problem that may well require integration across multiple systems. Or you may want to merge Web data on your customers with data from the order management module in your ERP system. Perhaps you want to combine data from your organization with market share or customer satisfaction data from an external supplier. Again, most organizations can't escape the need for data integration.

Stage 5 companies define and maintain key data elements such as customer, product, and supplier identifiers throughout the organization. Hence, they avoid complaints of, "Why can't I get a list of our top one hundred customers?" or "Why do I get different answers every time I ask how many employees we have?" It takes constant vigilance to have integrated, high-quality data. Citigroup's Institutional Bank (not necessarily a stage 5 firm at analytics overall, but very strong at customer data management) established a unique identifier for corporate customers in 1974, and has been refining it ever since. It maintains a group of data analysts in Manila to continually classify, tag, clean, and refine information about customers. Even though Citi's Institutional Bank—like most business-to-business organizations—has a relatively small number of customers, it's not easy to keep track of which organizations are parents and which are subsidiaries, or of name, location, and ownership changes. And it's a real nightmare if your organization has millions of consumers as customers.

In data integration, pundits often advocate "one version of the truth." You probably know the syndrome behind this recommendation. Several different groups come to a meeting to discuss something-or-other, each camp armed with facts to support its position. Sales are up for this reason, new hires are down for that reason, and so on. Trouble is, each group's data has different numbers for revenues, profits, total employees, daily moving average of cafeteria profits, you name it. The groups then spend more time arguing about whose data is correct and less time analyzing and acting on it.

The problem is indeed debilitating and worthy of attention. But you must narrow your focus: instead of attempting the Sisyphean task of cleaning up every data object in the company, select the master (or reference) data used in decision making and analysis. Employing certain processes and technologies to manage data objects (like customer, product, etc.) that are commonly used across the organization is called master data management, or MDM. MDM gets a bad reputation partly because it is rather unglamorous work. Just like eating your vegetables, managing your master data is good for you but not always satisfying or fun.

Furthermore, companies often make MDM a lot more complicated than it needs to be. According to Wikipedia (*Encyclopedia Britannica* and *Webster's* don't weigh in on this arcane subject—as of this writing, at least), MDM "has the objective of providing processes for collecting, aggregating, matching, consolidating, quality-assuring, persisting and distributing such data throughout an organization in such a way as to ensure consistency and control in the ongoing maintenance and application use of this information."

That gerund-rich definition suggests that MDM is a big hassle, and it is when MDM morphs into an unending data purification ordeal. Still, key data items do need to be defined in a common fashion and policed so they don't vary across the organization. So just be selective and start small. Focus on a pressing problem where cleaning some limited set of financial or customer data will bring a sizable payoff. Standardize data definitions and eliminate or correct incomplete, inaccurate, and inconsistent data. Then improve the lax data management and governance processes that caused the data to become dirty. When done, move on to other important chunks of data.

Ultimately you need to set a balance between integration efforts and analytical initiatives. If you embark on an MDM project, make sure you have plenty of money, time, and executive support. There's a pretty good chance that at some point during your MDM project somebody is going to say, "What the hell is master data management, and why's it taking so long and costing so much?" It would be good to have an answer at the ready.

In summary, stage 5 organizations have some data integration in place, but the perfect, flawlessly integrated, data-managed company is largely a fantasy. Even the best organizations don't have perfect data everywhere. They focus their data integration where it really makes a difference to their performance. The business need should drive the data integration efforts, not "just in case" mass integration or a misguided search for perfection.[6] Your targets for analytical work, as discussed in chapter 5, will steer you toward integration of the data that matters most.

Quality

Ironically, while data quality is important in analytical decision making, data doesn't have to be quite as perfect as it does in transactional systems or in basic business intelligence reporting applications. Skilled analysts can deal with missing data, and can even estimate substantial amounts of missing data or create statistical samples of data that get around the problem.

Nevertheless, flawed or misleading data is a problem for analytics. Having integrated data is only the first step. Keep in mind that most data is originally gathered for transactional purposes, not analytical ones. And every type of transactional data can have its own specific problems. Web transaction data, for example, can be plagued with problems that may inhibit your ability to extract meaningful analytics from your Web server logs. One Web analytics expert, Judah Phillips, identified eighteen glitches, ranging from spiders and bots that crawl your site and inflate your visit counts, to untagged pages that generate uncounted page views.[7]

With a particular decision and use of analytics in mind, analysts may need to trace data problems back to the source—often to the point where the data was originally entered—to find the root cause and to fix incorrect data. Even high-quality, integrated source systems like a modern ERP can't prevent front-line employees from entering data incorrectly. You may have to undertake some detective work to identify persistent sources of poor-quality data.

Stage 5 companies don't have perfectly clean data, but they have addressed many of their glaring data quality problems. They have data of sufficient quality for analytics in areas that really matter to their decision making. If they are focused on customer analytics, they have a high-quality customer database that has very few duplicated, inactive, or dead customers (the dead don't tend to respond well even to targeted promotions). Many of the customers' addresses may be outdated, but such errors may not matter for analytical purposes. Stage 5 companies also have a well-defined, relatively painless process for improving the quality of data as needed. Moreover, they have good processes up front to capture and validate data, so there isn't much cleanup to do.

In the late 1990s, Montana State Fund, a quasi-government agency that issues workers compensation insurance, dealt with data quality and integration by borrowing tactics from data piracy prevention. The resulting data contents were often challenged, so in 2006 it began a new initiative that certifies key reports and analyses with digital watermarks. The watermarks indicate that the data within the reports—over seventeen hundred elements extracted from core applications—are the official versions and have been audited. Users can print out the reports with the watermark, but can't download the data without losing the watermark. Al Parisian, the head of IT and strategy for Montana State Fund, reports that the culture of the organization is evolving to embrace the vastly improved data platform: "I've been in meetings where people argued based on selected events and partial data. Other people there have said, 'You can't use those isolated examples. Here's a report based on all the data from that period.'" Parisian knew that the approach was working when he saw that behavior.

Access

Data must be accessible in order to be analyzed—that is, it must be separated from the transaction-oriented applications (like sales order management or general ledger) in which it was created, and located where analysts can actually find and manipulate it. Stage 5 companies provide access to data by creating a data warehouse. Many companies have proliferated warehouses and single-purpose "data marts," but since integration is critical for advanced analytics, stage 5 companies will most likely have an enterprise data warehouse (EDW)—one that cuts across multiple functions and business units—for key analytical applications to draw from.

An EDW contains all the information that you might want to analyze—both current and historical values. If you think this is vague as an "information requirements" definition, you're exactly right. Because of an EDW's all-inclusive nature, firms always have to add new data elements to their warehouses, such as external data from Nielsen or other third-party providers. Thus the warehouses usually end up being so big that they overwhelm casual users. Since the original idea of a data warehouse is to make data more accessible to nontechnical users, something of a contradiction is built into the notion of an EDW. Still, many organizations have them, and they are a more feasible avenue for analytics than working directly with transaction data.

Unlike EDWs, data marts are departmental versions of data warehouses and sometimes are created independently of IT.[8] Although department-based data marts can limit analytics by undercutting integration, they can still play a role by solving some of the size problems of EDWs. For example, if you are pretty sure that most of your financial analytics will be restricted to data in the finance data mart, you should be fine relying on that source alone.

While you're thinking about access, you may want to (or, more appropriately, have to) think about speed. If you're going to be doing a lot of analytics you may need a special "data warehouse appliance." This dedicated system of software and hardware is optimized to do rapid queries and analytics. If you need your answers to analytical questions fast, you'll probably need such an appliance.

Some organizations have concluded that they don't need to—or can't afford to—make all their data available for analysis. If you have lots of different transaction systems and data sources on customers, for example, creating an entire customer information file would be very difficult. What these organizations have done might be called the "10 percent solution." They've taken a sample—most commonly 10 percent—of data for a particular domain—usually customers—and made that accessible for analysis. Such samples of large data populations can be very satisfactory for some analyses. A large bank did this as an early step toward building a customer data warehouse, and was able to make significant progress on analytical issues such as segmentation and promotion targeting. The data sampling strategy may also be useful as a pilot of an enterprise approach when business units are very independent and it's not clear whether managing data at the enterprise level will be feasible or effective.

Privacy

Highly analytical organizations tend to gather a lot of information about the entities they care about most—usually customers, but sometimes employees or business partners. Then they guard it with their lives. Stage 5 firms follow the Hippocratic oath of information privacy: above all, they do no harm. They have well-defined privacy policies about customer and employee information. They don't break the privacy laws of the territories or industries in which they operate (and that's not easy for a global company, because policies vary widely; Europe's laws are particularly strict). They don't lose information because of hackers or careless mistakes. They don't sell or give away information without the permission of the customer or employee. They get the information in the first place through "opt in" policies—that is, customers or employees give explicit permission for the information to be captured and used. They have clear restrictions about the frequency of customer contacts— they don't ever want to be viewed as pests by their customers. And if there is any doubt about when a particular analytical activity might cross the line of propriety, they don't cross it.

It's not just about having effective privacy policies, however. Stage 5 firms work with customer contact employees to ensure that they don't reveal sensitive information to or about customers. For example, one of Tesco's Clubcard loyalty card customers called the retailer's call center to complain about having received a coupon for condoms. Tesco often sends customers coupons based on what they have bought in the past, a fact that this customer seemed to know. "Does this mean," she asked, "that someone has bought condoms using my card?" The call center rep protected private information by coolly replying, "Sometimes we just send out coupons randomly," even though it was apparent from database records that condoms had been purchased using the customer's Clubcard number. In doing so, the service rep may also have saved a marriage, a feat to which every analytical practitioner should aspire.

Governance

Our discussions thus far may have suggested that data gets where it needs to be through supernatural forces. Alas, it is we imperfect humans who must manage data. And the term *governance* suggests that some humans are more important than others in managing it. For us, governance means all the ways that people ensure that data is useful for analysis: it is consistently defined, of sufficient quality, standardized, integrated, and accessible. Of course, one could argue that ensuring that an organization has good data is everyone's job, but that will guarantee that it's nobody's job. There are certain roles that need to be played if an organization wants to have stage 5 analytics. We'll describe the most important: executive decision makers, owners/stewards, and analytical data advocates.

Executive Decision Makers. Getting the organization aligned regarding the key data to be used in analytical projects is a job for senior managers. At a minimum, they must decide which information needs to be defined and managed in common across how much of the business. For example, if customers are to be a main analytical focus (probably the most common data domain for analytical work), senior executives must agree on a common term and meaning for "customer" throughout the organization. Most executive teams don't discuss information in this fashion, but their organization will not be able to integrate its data successfully without such deliberations.

High-level decisions about data also can only be made by senior management. Even if they are not comfortable with issues like ownership, stewardship, and relationship to strategy, they are the only ones who can deliberate about such matters. Since all data can't be perfect, only senior leaders can decide what kind of data—customer, product, supplier, zodiac sign, and so forth—is most critical to the organization's success. They will have to discuss what kinds of data assets correspond to particular strategic and analytical targets. Finally, they have to sign the checks for investments in data, so they will ultimately have to decide on major data-related programs and initiatives. If you're an IT or analytics person responsible for managing data, you need to engage your senior executives, or your lack of a relationship with upper management will come back to bite you.

Owners/Stewards. Many organizations will need to define specialized responsibilities for particular types of data—customer data, financial data, product data, and so on. Ownership is a highly loaded term that is likely to cause political difficulty and resentment; stewardship is a better term that avoids raising hackles. Stewardship entails taking responsibility for all the factors that make data useful to the business. This would typically be the job—perhaps full time, but more frequently part time—of business managers rather than IT people.

BMO (Bank of Montreal) Financial Group has adopted information stewardship to a large degree. BMO executives feel that the bank owns all of its information, but that they "need Business Information Stewards to ensure that it is managed appropriately across processes and functions."[9] BMO gives its stewards the following responsibilities:

- *Business definitions and standards.* Consistent interpretation of information and ability to integrate.

- *Information quality.* Accuracy, consistency, timeliness, validity, and completeness of information.

- *Information protection.* Appropriate controls to address security and privacy requirements.

- *Information life cycle.* Treatment of information from creation or collection through to retention or disposal.

BMO specifies particular stewardship functions at the strategic level (e.g., "Develop an information strategy and high-level 3–5 year plan"), the operational level (e.g., "Develop an information management change management strategy and program"), and the tactical level ("Develop, deliver, and maintain information operating procedures to support the information management corporate standards"). Information stewards at BMO are business executives, and the stewardship role is typically part time.

Analytical Data Advocates. While IT organizations are usually skilled at building data infrastructures and installing and maintaining applications that generate transaction data, they are not often oriented to helping the organization use data in reporting and analytical processes. One way to ensure that focus is to create a group that emphasizes information management and ensures that data and information can easily be accessed and analyzed. Such groups are becoming increasingly common; some call them business intelligence competency centers (BICCs).[10]

Other organizations with slightly broader objectives than facilitating business intelligence refer to their "analytical data advocate" group as information management (IM) or business information management. Two organizations that have established such groups are the health insurer Humana and the South African banking unit of Barclays, Absa Bank.

Humana's group is responsible for information management and "informatics," the term health care organizations use for analytics for patient care and disease management. One of the group's first priorities was to develop a strategy, enlisting the support of senior executives throughout the organization. Lisa Tourville, the head of the group, reports to the firm's chief financial officer, although her group addresses all sorts of information—not just financial. Lisa has a strong actuarial background, and describes her personal vision as "to be an advocate of all matters quantitative and relentlessly search to improve analytic capabilities in support of corporate decision-making efforts."[11] That's a great set of goals for the head of such a group.

Absa Bank established its IM group in 2001, and was initially focused on customer information. David Donkin, the first head of the IM group, explained the group's mission: allow information- and knowledge-based strategy formulation and decision making, and leverage information to improve business performance. These are at the heart of what it takes to make an organization more analytical.

The IM group at Absa is responsible for the data warehouses, BI tools and applications, data mining, and geographic information systems. IM also develops the bank's information strategy and architecture, which defines how the bank stores and manipulates information. Donkin has represented Absa at broader gatherings of Barclays' analytical community. The corporate IT organization manages Absa's operational applications, databases, and the IT and network architecture.

According to Donkin, when the IM group was formed, Absa's data warehouse was "not customer centric, not operationally stable, and not business directed." It stored information that no one really needed, and that few knew how to find. Today the IM group improves the relationship between IT at the back end and business decision makers on the front end. It facilitates such analytical applications as scorecards, fraud detection, risk management, and customer analytics, which drive cross-sell, up-sell, retention, customer segmentation, and lifetime value scores.[12]

Even if you have a BICC or an IM group, you can never do enough connecting between IT and rest of the business. Whether the group is separate from or part of the IT organization, you must have some data people in IT who are familiar with the typical types of analysis done in your industry and company. If they know that, they can help to ensure that the data is structured for easy access and analysis.

Data Before Analytics

Getting data in order is so critical to analytics that most organizations have to undertake substantial data management efforts before they can do a lot of analysis. For example, at Albert Heijn, the largest supermarket chain in the Netherlands with over eight hundred stores, considerable data efforts were undertaken to create the ability to do analytics.

In the 1990s, Albert Heijn embarked on a program of differentiating stores along several dimensions such as assortments, replenishments, targeted customer segments, and so forth. To accomplish this objective while maintaining cost parity, Albert Heijn's managers concluded that it needed a more integrated data environment. They developed a blueprint of the company's envisioned information environment, covering and integrating data from the total value chain, resulting in an enterprise data warehouse. Previously Albert Heijn had a great deal of data, but it was spread across a number of different systems and databases. The goal was one integrated environment for all enterprise processes and transactions, using the most granular data possible and supporting the entire company. Albert Heijn embarked upon a multiyear data integration project that ultimately cost €30 million.

The resulting database was called PALLAS, after the Greek goddess of knowledge (a classical name adds class to data integration projects). It eventually drew from 75 percent of the company's transaction systems and contained ten years of online detailed data. Over three thousand employees now run reports from the data or perform analysis, and each week over sixty thousand customers use the system to see what items they recently bought. Management questions on store operations can be answered nearly in real time. Forecasts of store demand for particular items, for example, are updated every five minutes, and stores are automatically replenished based on the forecasts.

Once PALLAS was created and the initial demand for reporting satisfied, Albert Heijn began to turn its attention to analytics. It formed a business analytics group to perform analytical projects across the organization and professionalize the area of analytics within the company. It is also using sophisticated artificial intelligence technologies rarely seen in retail. Single-purpose data marts created over the years support analysis in particular domains. The first one involved replenishment, with the goal of reducing stockouts and shrinkage of inventory. Now a variety of analytical projects are under way using PALLAS data, including projects on loyalty, assortment optimization, promotion analysis, and introduction of nonfood items to Albert Heijn stores. These projects wouldn't have been possible without the availability of integrated, high-quality data.

Data Through the Stages

We've described a number of attributes of the most sophisticated analytical competitors. What if you don't aspire to that level of analytical orientation? How can the opera houses, circus colleges, and other businesses of the world make analytics work for them? The remainder of the chapter addresses what organizations do with data at lower levels of analytical focus, and how they can move to the next step. Table 2-1 provides an overview of these transitions.

TABLE 2-1

Moving to the next stage: Data

From stage 1 *Analytically Impaired* to stage 2 *Localized Analytics*	From stage 2 *Localized Analytics* to stage 3 *Analytical Aspirations*	From stage 3 *Analytical Aspirations* to stage 4 *Analytical Companies*	From stage 4 *Analytical Companies* to stage 5 *Analytical Competitors*
Gain mastery over local data of importance, including building functional data marts.	Build enterprise consensus around some analytical targets and their data needs. Build some domain data warehouses (e.g., customer) and corresponding analytical expertise. Motivate and reward cross-functional data contributions and management.	Build enterprise data warehouses and integrate external data. Engage senior executives in EDW plans and management. Monitor emerging data sources.	Educate and engage senior executives in competitive potential of analytical data. Exploit unique data. Establish strong data governance, especially stewardship. Form a BICC if you don't have one yet.

From Stage 1 to Stage 2. The story from stage 1 to stage 2 is about basic data mastery, usually the prerequisite missing in stage 1 companies. If it's available at all, data is inconsistent and of poor quality. Therefore, to move to stage 2, particular functions need to create the necessary data from capable transaction systems, and make it available for analysis purposes. There are no enterprise data warehouses at this stage, but we may see the beginning of functional data marts or operational data stores.

In moving from stage 1 to stage 2, all analytical activities, including those involving data, tend to start and remain at the local level. Functional or business units marshal the necessary data and analysts to undertake analytical initiatives in their areas. There are many different targets throughout the organization, so there is little or no ability for the enterprise to focus on data hygiene and accessibility projects.

From Stage 2 to Stage 3. Now senior executives show signs of interest in analytics, encouraging analytical and data-oriented people from around the organization to start communicating and collaborating. The key here is to create some successes with data—identifying new sources, extracting some from transaction databases, buying it externally, and using it for analytical purposes. There is also the beginning of organizational consensus on a key analytical target, and some recognition that data needs to be integrated and shared.

An enterprise-level target allows the organization to begin focusing data initiatives in subject areas that support future analytical strategies. For example, if a company believes its primary future lies in customer analytics, building a customer data warehouse is the first order of business. Similarly, creating human expertise around customer data and analytics should be a priority. If the long-term vision involves something else—product data or claims data or genomic data or what have you—then the initial focus should be in that area.

In transitioning from stage 2 to stage 3, data and other resources begin to be viewed as organizational, rather than departmental, resources. Enterprise-level data strategies begin to appear. Functional or business unit managers who have built up data capabilities may be either threatened or, ideally, flattered by the adoption of their data and analysis approaches by the organization at large. Therefore, solid—not necessarily passionate—leadership at the enterprise level is necessary to get to this stage. Local owners of data need to be rewarded for giving it up, or have their wrists slapped for holding on to it.

From Stage 3 to Stage 4. In stage 3 the organization has a long-term vision of where it wants to go with analytics, but for some reason feels the goal is not achievable in the short run. The key in moving to stage 4, then, is to facilitate the organization's efforts to create tangible analytical projects at the enterprise level. From a data standpoint, the focus must be on building cross-functional data capabilities. This means that organizations need to replace function-level data marts with an enterprise-level warehouse. The data in the warehouse will come mostly from internal transactional systems, but increasingly from integrating internal and external data. To justify and pay for these activities, senior managers will have to be engaged and consulted on data issues.

We've found several organizations whose long-term vision involves using data that simply isn't practical to gather today. For example, health care institutions and pharmaceutical firms see a future of "personalized medicine" in which drugs are based on a patient's genomic and proteomic profile. Today, that information is both expensive and difficult to manage. So it's crucial to watch the development of the needed data to see when it will be available, and perhaps to institute a pilot project to analyze the data available now—so that you will know what to do with it when it finally arrives.

From Stage 4 to Stage 5. How do stage 5 companies differ from stage 4? Stage 4 organizations are generally competent at managing data and have most of the required data resources in place. They have adequate transaction systems, data warehouses, and perhaps even some nonnumerical content. However, because these firms are not yet passionate about using the data for competitive purposes, they have not optimized their data environments for analysis. They probably do not have a strong focus on unique data for their industry. They may not have governance functions in place to mediate between business-side analysts and decision makers, and people in the IT organization who are data infrastructure providers for analytical projects.

Since the primary difference between stage 4 and stage 5 organizations is a passion for analytics, the key step in that transition is to excite senior executives about analytical possibilities. We're not suggesting the implementation of a weekly Algorithm Appreciation Day, but educational activities for an organization's leaders can emphasize the role of well-managed and differentiated data in an analytically focused strategy—with as many examples as possible of competitors and other firms that have used data for competitive advantage. A simple assessment of key data resources around the organization may help to stimulate thinking and action.

In terms of governance, it may be useful to pilot some stewardship or business-side information management functions, or to select a friendly executive as an initial steward. It may also be advisable to create a small business intelligence competency center.

Skipping Steps or Accelerating Progress

In the data space, it would certainly be possible to skip a step or two, or move quickly through a stage. If you're now in stage 1 and want to become a more analytical enterprise, it would definitely be a good idea to skip the silo-based approach of stage 2. If your executive team will support a cross-functional, enterprise-oriented approach, it makes good sense to begin building an enterprise data warehouse, for example. However, since you'll need some sense of where to focus your efforts, you need the targets and vision that typically come only with engaged executives at stage 3.

It probably wouldn't work to skip from stage 1 or 2 to stage 4 or 5. Putting the data infrastructure in place—along with the human infrastructure relative to data, analysis, and analytical strategy—takes time. Further, many of the investments necessary to move along the maturity curve for analytics may not be supported by executives until they see evidence of value from early projects. However, if you have a very supportive CEO and executive team, you can make progress quickly.

Keep in Mind . . .

- Have someone in your data management organization who understands analytics and how to create them, and who can educate others about the differences between data for analytics and data for business transactions or reporting.

- If you can't obtain all the data for a particular subject area (e.g., customers), then create a statistically valid sample with a fraction of the data. In cases when you just need some directional insight, creating a sample is a lot faster and cheaper. In most cases, though, try to obtain as much detailed data as possible.

- Create an organization whose job it is to ensure that business information is well defined, well maintained, and well used.

- Identify data stewards, generally from outside IT, for key information content domains (customer, product, employee, etc.).

- Find some data that is unique and proprietary that your organization can exploit analytically.

- Experiment with nonnumerical data—video, social media, voice, text, scent, and so on. (Okay, maybe not scent, unless you're running a company that deals in personal hygiene.)

- Don't spend all your time and resources on achieving perfection with data completeness, quality, or integration—save time for analysis!

3

ENTERPRISE

Integrating Across Organizational Silos

YES, WE KNOW we just gave you an entire chapter on data, but stay with us for one more example. A major multinational ventured out to become an analytical company in 2006 by launching OneData—a global initiative to manage information as a critical, competitive asset. The initiative encouraged the company to draw on, as on executive put it, "one source of truth" to fuel better business insights and, ultimately, better business decisions. The OneData program grasped an important principle about analytics: the opposite of an enterprisewide perspective isn't a local or independent perspective, but a *fractured* one. To develop an enterprisewide view of analytics, a company must do more than integrate data combine analysts, or build a corporate IT platform. It must eradicate all of the limited, piecemeal perspectives harbored by managers with their own agendas, needs, and fears—and replace them with a single, holistic view of the company. It may sound like we're proselytizing for a Far Eastern cult, but this is really just an effective management practice.

Without a broad business perspective, a company cannot address the strategic issues at the core of business performance and organizational competitiveness. Vital management questions may go unanswered if information is fragmented:

- Which performance factors have the greatest impact on our future growth and profitability?

- How can we anticipate and influence changing market conditions?

- If customer satisfaction improves, what is the impact on profitability? Is customer loyalty more important than, for instance, order volume?

- How should we optimize investments across our products, geographies, and marketing channels?

- Are managers' decisions well aligned with our company strategy, or are they merely promoting the managers' self-interest?

Analytics can illuminate these high-level questions only if decision makers can see across regions, business units, or processes and consider information from the entire enterprise. Furthermore, an enterprise perspective ensures that analytical data and models are treated with intellectual honesty. Without strict standards enforced from the top, the temptation to filter assumptions and risks through narrower, self-serving perspectives may be too great.

Strategic concerns like performance and risk aren't the only reasons to adopt an enterprise perspective; a coordinated approach also improves analytical activities in business processes and functions, including IT. Without an analytics strategy and road map, most IT organizations will struggle to anticipate and support business requirements. Lacking direction, project managers will be assigned to initiatives that produce little value, missing opportunities to work on useful projects. IT will default to supporting the easy analytics projects, or those for which they already have the data, or those with the squeakiest wheels. Even worse, they may admit defeat and supply whatever data they can get their hands on, hoping some of it will be useful. Merck executive Robin DeHaan summarizes the pitfalls of this fractured approach: "The repercussions are more ad hoc activity, more fire drills, and more spin-off databases . . . Expediency overrides strategy."[1]

Without central coordination, business unit or functional managers will attempt to build their own analytic fiefdoms, as was the case at one midwestern health care provider network. A vice president and a director there told us about analytics projects that are scattered among four groups and seven hospitals, networkwide projects that lack strong ownership, and top managers in the hospitals who do as they please with little oversight. As a result, they complained, it's hard to break analytics efforts out of institutional silos: "Nobody knows who knows what. Even as basic a task as creating a central data warehouse with all that scattered information is like recreating the federal government."

Duplicated efforts also lead to conflict and errors. Infighting breaks out between executives or groups of employees using different systems and data sources, because when their numbers and analysts inevitably disagree, each side claims its analyses are right. These analytical Montagues and Capulets operate at cross-purposes, undermining or competing with each other instead of cooperating.

A coordinated enterprise approach also reduces complexity. Absent knowledge of the company's analytical needs—or even which projects are under way or in the planning stage—business analysts may buy the same data or software that others in the organization have already bought. Thus, hundreds of data marts, reporting packages, forecasting tools, data management solutions, integration tools, and methodologies spring up like mushrooms. One firm we know of had 275 data marts and a thousand different information resources, but couldn't pull together a single view of the business in terms of key performance metrics and customer data. Often, it is harder to rein in all this activity than it would have been to coordinate it in the first place. Best Buy, for example, realized that by streamlining the 293 analytical systems and data feeds that had proliferated when the company began to adopt analytics, it could improve quality and cut costs.

Two-thirds of large U.S. companies believe they need to improve their enterprise's analytical capabilities. And even though more than half (57 percent) of the companies we surveyed said they lack a consistently updated, enterprisewide analytical capability, nearly three-quarters (70 percent) said they are working to increase their company's business analytics usage.[2]

Most CIOs recognize that only an enterprise IT strategy will derive real value from analytics. This same study found that 75 percent wanted to see an end to silos of information and 76 percent of CIOs planned to develop an enterprise business intelligence strategy over the next three years. But while their support was strong, more than half acknowledged that their company still lacked an enterprise approach to analytics.

If you're not a CIO, it may be natural to keep your head down and focus on what's in your own sphere of control. But that approach leads to bad decisions and self-serving projects, not judicious, enterprise-serving programs. Our advice: take an enterprise-minded approach right from the outset of your analytical journey. Even in a stage 1 company, it's best to look ahead, think about the future upsides and potential downsides to the enterprise, and treat even local, departmental projects as potential bases for broader initiatives.

How Much Integration and Coordination Are Needed for Enterprise Analytics?

Corporations can be diverse and far-flung. We spoke with one diversified financial services provider who grapples with this question: "To what extent should we integrate our data, analyses, and processes across our enterprise when we have so many different types of customers, operate in so many different markets, offer so many different kinds of products, and operate in a volatile economic environment where we are making regular acquisitions and divestures?" This is really the question of what is meant by "enterprise" in particular organizations.

Consider General Electric. It sells wind turbines, auto loans, jet engines, washing machines, fluorescent lightbulbs, and commercial airtime on *Saturday Night Live*. Does data about its wind turbine clients in Germany and its washing machine customers in Thailand need to be shared across the entire corporation? Do customer analytics apply across those organizational boundaries? Probably not. But in some areas—such as talent management and volume purchase agreements—GE should share data from several or even all of its businesses. And by initiating a common and central analytical capability across its GE Capital financial services business, GE is taking the first step toward an enterprise perspective at that level.

How you adopt an enterprise perspective for analytics depends on the answer to one question: who else in my company could be interested in the same data, technology, and analytics now or in the future? Any group in a corporation that shares or could share customers, markets, inventory, and suppliers, or any group that participates in the same analytical projects based on those business entities, should be considered part of a single enterprise. When in doubt, ask if any other groups need common data to answer any of the six analytical questions in figure 1-1. If they do, there is value in aligning common technical infrastructure, data, definitions, analytics, and decision processes.

Sometimes a business network shares information across multiple enterprises. Wal-Mart is famous for sharing data with its suppliers, with the expectation that suppliers will use the information to lower prices and increase sales in partnership with the retailer. According to a 2006 Accenture study, 24 percent of organizations had such direct linkages with customers and 15 percent had them with suppliers.[3] A company that is committed to helping its customers and suppliers make better decisions will have to share not only data, but also analytics and analytical expertise, to create its "extended enterprise."

Determining the best level of alignment or integration across business units is particularly tricky at a global conglomerate or after a merger, when it may be impractical to treat separate businesses and geographic units as a single entity. Executives at Air France/KLM describe themselves as one company, two airlines, and three businesses: passenger, cargo, and maintenance. So from an analytics perspective, are they one, two, or three different enterprises? Our six questions in figure 1-1 can provide some clarity. For example, the answer to "What's the best that can happen?" may suggest optimizing the airline crews or maintenance staff by looking across both airlines.

But sometimes data must be left in its silo for practical or legal reasons. We wouldn't expect a winery like Gallo to launch a national "frequent wine drinker" program, for example. The laws covering the sale and distribution of liquor vary too much from state to state, and even from county to county, to make such a promotion possible (and it would be tacky).[4] Also, companies that regularly acquire and sell off businesses probably would not treat their subsidiaries' data as part of one enterprise; it's simpler to spin them off if their data, systems, and decisions aren't intertwined.

Organizations that are served by different IT functions can have so much difficulty sharing data and IT infrastructure that, as a practical matter, they can't be unified under the same enterprise. Geographically based IT departments in a diverse multinational company are a common obstacle to adopting an enterprise perspective. In other cases, the need for an enterprise approach may evolve with shifts in corporate strategy. One diversified European products company, for example, had a history of treating business units independently, but as the company sought synergies across its products, they developed a more unified information management vision.

How IT Enables an Enterprise Perspective

As we noted earlier, most CIOs have good intentions when it comes to developing an enterprise information strategy. That's good news for any manager hoping to nudge his or her company down the path to fact-based decision making. But as the cop directing traffic on the road to hell will tell you, good intentions can lead to unhappy endings. IT has to deliver on its aspirations.

CIOs and their IT organizations still have two big jobs to do. The first is to stay focused on supporting the analytics work that matters most; IT organizations have historically focused on transactional applications, leaving little time and money for the more crucial task of data analysis. The second job is to build an IT infrastructure capable of delivering the information and analytics that people across the enterprise need, now and into the future.[5] IT must resist the temptation to provide analytics as an add-on or bolt-on to whatever transaction system it just developed. Unless the IT organization builds a platform that can standardize and integrate data, provide users with the applications they need, and adapt as needs and strategies change, analytics won't be able to scale to the enterprise level.

In the early stages of analytics, IT organizations are apt to take a hands-off approach. They provide reports much the same way the proprietor of a self-service station sells gasoline: the selection is limited, and the customers pump their own. Self-service isn't a bad idea in the beginning if it gives information workers ready access to standard reporting and frees up IT resources to focus on other tasks. But in the later stages of analytics—stages 4 and 5—IT needs to shift gears from self-service operator to proactive advocate and architect for change. IT should do what it takes to help decision makers get the data and technology they need and to generate the insights that help them decide effectively. Ultimately, IT should become part owner of the company's analytical capabilities, and business leaders should make this expectation clear.

IT managers must understand and be able to articulate the potential of analytics for the enterprise. If they don't have an enterprise perspective, they won't be able to build an enterprise reality. IT staff should interact with the analytical pros who build models and the analytical amateurs who use them and consume their information: the greater the interaction, the clearer the understanding of the business potential and risks on both sides. And speaking of understanding, IT managers make their own lives easier when they close the language gap that separates them from their business colleagues: instead of talking to executives about things like clouds, SOA, and OLAP, they should talk about decision making, insights, and business performance.

Building an enterprise IT platform for analytics can be a long, intimidating road. But like every journey, it starts with a single step. It begins with good, integrated data on transactions and business processes managed through enterprise applications like ERP and CRM systems. But it doesn't end there. An Accenture study on how companies use enterprise systems found that the companies that derived any real value from them had *anticipated* how to leverage the information to generate new insights to improve business performance.[6]

These initial steps increase the likelihood of success. Stage 5 organizations develop a robust information management environment that provides an enterprisewide set of systems, applications, and governance processes. They begin by eliminating legacy systems and old spaghetti code and then press forward to eliminate silos of information like data marts and spreadsheet marts. They hunt for pockets of standalone analytic applications and either migrate them to centralized analytic applications or shut them down.

Analytical companies also experiment with emerging analytical tools. For example, Procter & Gamble piloted a short-term demand forecasting tool for inventory optimization from Terra Technology, a recent start-up. P&G found that the new software could decrease short-term forecast error by more than 30 percent. The company estimates that the predictive tool will yield more than $100 million in increased cash flow globally.[7] Draftfcb, a global integrated marketing communications agency, experiments with a variety of tools to deliver analytical insights and results to clients and agency colleagues. Its analytical professionals use multiple tools for analytical data visualization and illustrating relationships among brand concepts, including Flash and open-source tools. They note that being successful with analytics is not just about the data or the advanced techniques they utilize, but about telling the story and making it visually appealing.[8] Without an enterprise-level group to explore such tools, it's unlikely that Draftfcb would be able to employ such capabilities.

Finally, we mustn't overlook the analytical tools and applications themselves. Formerly small, independent analytics vendors like Business

Objects, Cognos, and Hyperion are being consolidated and integrated into the major players (such as Oracle, Microsoft, SAP, SAS, and IBM). Standardizing around an enterprisewide software suite helps ensure a consistent approach to data management, and provides an integrated environment complete with the data repositories, analytical tools, presentation applications, and transformation tools ready to be incorporated into improved business processes.

As they shift from point solutions to enterprise software suites, software vendors continue to seek innovative ways to embed analytics into business processes and workflow. Data warehouse providers are augmenting basic SQL query capabilities with analytical functionality such as prediction, regression, decision trees, clustering, and Bayesian analysis. And business applications are becoming more analytically sophisticated as customers demand better insight into operational decisions.

If you are an analytics user or advocate, this long list of IT requirements may be overwhelming. But fortunately, building an enterprise platform is IT's job, not yours. Your job is to watch out for current and future users of the information and systems. Keep up with the IT people; ask direct questions and demand results to make sure that your company constructs the accessible, well-managed analytical resources it needs. But be patient: it may take several iterations to get it all right.

An Enterprise Approach to Analysts

The enterprise orientation applies not only to data and IT, but also to the people who do analytical work. Pockets and silos of analytical people are just as problematic as the other types of pockets and silos we've discussed in this chapter. However, we're going to ask you to read "Organizing Analysts" in chapter 6, which is about analysts in general. If you can't wait, we suppose you could skip ahead now—but that would be a bit rash.

Enterprise Perspective Through the Stages

In a true stage 5 company, awareness of analytics is enterprisewide. Analytics are embedded in everyday business processes, so managers and employees in every business unit can make fact-based decisions. The enterprise is continually evolving, finding new ways to use analytics and inventing new tools as it reinvents its business processes. The entire business is served by a flexible, centralized IT infrastructure designed for analytical excellence. All this comes under the aegis of an enterprise strategy development and performance management process, where strategy is made with analytics in mind. Executives and employees throughout understand why analytics are important, how they fit into the company strategy, and where the risks lie—and they are eager to exploit this knowledge.

Table 3-1 summarizes how an enterprise approach evolves over each stage.

From Stage 1 to Stage 2. At stage 1, there's no enterprise view, interest, or capacity for analytics. But the need is there. A few scattered workers, maybe newcomers to the company, have problems to solve or decisions to make but can't get the information they need out of the existing corporate systems. They are itching to get their hands on some good, clean data. Out of necessity, these organizational Swiss Family Robinsons may even build their own little ad hoc analytical application on the sly, using whatever information they can scrape up. This is where the long, hard climb toward enterprise analytics begins. If you're a lonely proponent of analytics, your job is first to get managers to sponsor analytic

TABLE 3-1

Moving to the next stage: Enterprise

From stage 1 Analytically Impaired to stage 2 Localized Analytics	From stage 2 Localized Analytics to stage 3 Analytical Aspirations	From stage 3 Analytical Aspirations to stage 4 Analytical Companies	From stage 4 Analytical Companies to stage 5 Analytical Competitors
Find allies for small-scale analytics projects that nonetheless suggest cross-functional or enterprise potential. Manage data risk at local level. Partner with IT on common tool selection and data standards.	Select applications with relevance to multiple business areas. Keep scope manageable, but with an eye to future expansion. Establish standards for data privacy and security. Begin building enterprise analytical infrastructure incrementally.	Develop analytics strategy and road map for major business unit, if not the enterprise. Conduct risk assessments of all analytical applications. Establish enterprise governance of technology and architecture for analytics.	Manage analytical priorities and assets at the enterprise level. Implement enterprisewide model review and management. Extend analytics tools and infrastructure broadly and deeply across the enterprise.

projects and later to convince skeptics of their value. You will find allies for your nonviolent revolution in disgruntled managers with unmet information needs and supporters in IT managers who get excited about your plans. Once you have this backing, develop a business case for small-scale, easily attainable, "low-hanging fruit" analytics projects. Promise to share the information and the credit for success, to track ROI, and to keep the information secure. You've reached stage 2 when these demonstration projects start getting approved, and you should start to anticipate what an enterprise approach to analytics might look like.

From Stage 2 to Stage 3. Jump ahead a few months or years. By now, the first analytics projects have proven their worth, and the CEO and some other executives have noticed them. Your goal is to start planning a well-focused enterprise analytics capability. At this juncture, a few forward-thinking companies may start to standardize their IT platform for analytics, but most will plan first.

Here's what to do. First, define the concept of "enterprise," and work with your organization's executives to develop a vision of what you can do with analytics. Later, identify the best strategic targets and projects; finally, identify your desired benefits and the means to measure them. Expect to spend time scrutinizing performance data to identify the levers that drive business performance. Assess your enterprise's current capabilities: its skills, its business processes, its ability to manage analytics' risks, and its technology. What are they now, and what do they need to be?

As you plan, educate executives on the risks of analytics and be sure you don't overreach. Treat each project as a demonstration that has to win over the inevitable skeptics. And be ready for infighting and hard negotiating. Chances are, your plans will threaten some managers— particularly if your organization isn't generally geared toward making fact-based and analytical decisions. Be ready to provide skeptics with something they want in order to get what you want.

From Stage 3 to Stage 4. Now your company is moving from planning to implementing. Your company has singled out the most important strategic applications, and you are ready to start standardizing data and technology in earnest. At this stage, it's not uncommon for senior managers to advocate analytical decision making and to push back when they don't get it. Your organization is starting to act like an analytical enterprise rather than an analytical wannabe. Just be ready for several enterprisewide stress points. The first is putting in place the new IT infrastructure and standards. Create a road map for getting it done, and be sure it's implemented in a step-by-step manner; too much too fast means mistakes and resistance. The second stress point of enforcing your new data policies is also hard, since it means changing habits and calling out repeat offenders. At this stage you've started sharing common customer and process data among the stakeholders. They'll be anxious about losing control of the data to a central function, and confused as squabbles break out over how the data is defined and why the numbers differ. You may have to embark on a time-consuming "one version of the truth" project to reconcile a key information domain.

From Stage 4 to Stage 5. If your company has made it to stage 4, congratulations. You're already a Che Guevara of analytical uprisings. You're making analytical and fact-based decisions (but you're not as fanatical as Che). Now, if your executive team has become committed to turning your company into an analytical competitor, there's more work to be done. Chances are your organization still has stage 2 or 3 pockets in certain regions or business units; the time has come to bring them up to speed. You will need to revisit your IT architecture and infrastructure, see what further changes must be made to put analytics at its core, and implement them. All the skills and support functions for analytics—project management, analytical experts, IT support—are now enterprisewide groups. The most stressful changes affect rank and file business users and workers, who see their job descriptions and functions change as the company adopts a new way of doing business. The IT, HR, and operations groups need to bone up on their change management skills.

An enterprise analytics capacity requires more than integrating data or building a corporatewide IT platform to support analytics. It means replacing dozens of limited, fragmented perspectives of managers with their own agendas, needs, and fears with one far-seeing holistic view of how analytics can serve the company. Changing how people think about analytics and convincing them to overcome their limited views and their (sometimes limitless) fears can't be achieved by sending out a memo or installing a new system. It's a job that requires leadership—the next part of the DELTA model.

Keep in Mind . . .

- Seek out kindred spirits in IT and collaborate with other potential constituencies and stakeholders.

- Take responsibility for securing and ensuring the quality of enterprise data. That includes participating in data governance initiatives.

- Build your integrated analytical environment over time, not all at once.

- Inside the enterprise, manage toward an equilibrium of supply (data, technology, analysts) and demand for analytics.

4

LEADERSHIP

The Deciding DELTA Factor

IF WE HAD TO CHOOSE a single factor to determine how analytical an organization will be, it would be leadership. If leaders get behind analytical initiatives, they are much more likely to bear fruit. Leaders have a strong influence on culture and can mobilize people, money, and time to help push for more analytical decision making. A decade ago, when we did our first study on how companies build analytical capability, we concluded that one of the most important prerequisites is having leaders who care about analytical decision making—a conclusion that we still stand behind today.[1]

However, there is one revision we'd like to make to our earlier thinking, writing, and speaking: we focused, perhaps too narrowly, on analytical leadership from CEOs. Now, there is no doubt that to be a full-fledged analytical competitor, you need the CEO in your corner. However, there is also no doubt that almost any employee can move an organization in a more analytical direction. To be sure, an impressive title and massive resources help, but in this chapter we'll discuss how a variety of people who aren't CEOs can make their organizations more analytical and fact based.

We'll begin by focusing on the typical attributes of analytical leaders—the traits that help them move their organizations toward analytical decision making. If you want, you can probably use these as a sort of assessment to see how you—or someone you know—stacks up as an analytical leader. Some of the attributes are more likely to be found among high-level executives such as CEOs; others are more appropriate for lower- and midlevel managers and individual contributors.

Included in this chapter are four case studies of analytical leaders at different levels of organizations: the head of an analytical department, the head of a business function, a business unit head and entrepreneur, and a CEO/president team. We discuss how each leader exhibits many of the analytical leadership traits we've laid out. Even this broad range of leaders by no means covers the variety of leadership possibilities; almost anyone can help an organization to become more analytical, including individual contributors.

What Analytical Leaders Do

Analytical leaders at every level of the organization exhibit some common traits. Of course, almost no leader has them all, and different leaders have the traits in different proportions. But before talking about how they're embodied in real people, we think it's useful to lay out these attributes in the abstract.

Analytical leaders tend to demonstrate the following behaviors.

Develop Their People Skills. Analytical leaders need to have good people skills—a trait that is not as obvious as it sounds. Many highly analytical people seem to prefer computers and data to people; they don't sympathize, empathize, or communicate well with others. Why should they, if humans don't even come with a SORT function or an easily searchable interface? But if you don't have good people skills, you're not going to be a good leader of any type—including analytical.

Push for More Data and Analysis. The core responsibility of an analytical leader is to set the expectation that people will make decisions based on data and analysis. If someone comes to you with a recommendation that appears to be based on intuition, you'll push back if you're an analytical leader. You may encourage the miscreant to gather more data, relate it to some other data, perform a correlation analysis, or (assuming certain capabilities) build a multivariate probit regression model. If you let people get away with sloppy logic and uninformed intuition as their primary decision tools, they won't naturally move toward analytics and facts—tools that are harder to gather and use. Most people need a bit of urging to move in the analytical direction.

Hire Smart People, and Give Them Credit for Being Smart. One of the most important functions of analytical leaders is to hire smart analysts. Many companies in industries that have not previously been very analytical find themselves with relatively few people who can do serious analytical work, so they have to be brought in. Persuading quantitative MBAs or PhDs to work in places like Harrah's or Sears that have never had such people is a tall order. Once they are hired, good leaders provide a stimulating and supportive work environment for analysts and give them credit for the work that they do. We've all seen managers who present others' analyses in meetings as their own. These are not good analytical leaders—or good leaders at all.

Set a Hands-on Example. Analytical leaders aren't hypocrites. They lead by example, using data and analysis in their own decisions. This doesn't mean that they have to know all the details of Chi Square Automatic Interaction Detection (affectionately known as CHAID) or structural equation modeling. But they do need to have the same passion for fact-based decision making that they want to inspire in the people they lead. Occasionally, they'll feel the need to get their hands dirty and mess around with data and brainstorm with analysts themselves. They'll do so because they like analytics and because they want others to emulate their example.

Sign Up for Results. As Joe Megibow of Hotels.com points out, it's common to find middle- and lower-level analysts who complain about the lack of analytical leadership in their organizations. If only their work were appreciated! If only someone understood how important they were! But there is something they can do to take leadership. They can commit themselves to achieving a specific result in the part of the organization they serve or control. If they're in direct mail, they can take responsibility for a certain level of promotional lift. If they're in Web metrics, they can increase page views. If they're in supply chain, they can reduce inventory by a specified level. This will advance the analytical orientation of the organization overall, and probably get the person who signed up for the result a promotion if it's achieved. That's just what it did for Megibow, who was recently promoted to the senior analytical role at Expedia, the parent company of Hotels.com.

Teach. Analytical leaders are patient teachers of applying analytical perspectives to business. Sometimes they teach actual analytical techniques. At other times they gently guide employees and colleagues into more rigorous thinking and decision making. If you've received the best kind of teaching from analytical leaders, you may not even be aware that you've been taught—all of a sudden you have stretched your capabilities, and you think you've done it on your own.

Set Strategy and Performance Expectations. Good analytical leaders know that analytics and fact-based decisions don't happen in a vacuum. In order for people to know where and how to apply their analytical skills, they need a strategy for their business, function, and even department. What are we trying to accomplish? Which goals will analytics help to achieve? After setting the strategy, analytical leaders need to define a set of performance targets for their organizations and direct reports to achieve. Defining the metrics will itself drive the organization in a more analytical direction and motivate employees to begin using analytical tools themselves.

Look for Leverage. Since analytics can been applied to a variety of business problems, it's important to focus them where it makes a difference. Strong analytical leaders know where to find leverage—where a small improvement in a process driven by analytics can make a big difference. A simple example would be in retail, where a small improvement in profit margin or lift gets multiplied across many sales. One of the analytical leaders we describe in the following profiles, Tom Anderson, says that he looks for a "multiplicative" business—one in which a small analytical advantage gets multiplied through several different factors that drive business success.

Demonstrate Persistence Over Time. Analytical leaders have to be "pluggers"—people who work doggedly and persistently—because changes that apply analytics to decision making, business processes, information systems, culture, and strategy hardly happen overnight. Even once they do happen, leaders have to continually revise and update their analytical approaches. So if you want to be an analytical leader, be patient and be prepared to work at it for the long haul.

Build an Analytical Ecosystem. Analytical leaders can rarely go it alone in building analytical capabilities. Instead, they have to build an ecosystem consisting of other leaders in their business, employees, external analytical suppliers, business partners, and so forth. The networks supply talent, advice, resources, tools, and solutions to common problems. In effect, leadership comes not from individuals, but from a network of analytical leaders across organizations.

Work Along Multiple Fronts. Analytical leaders know that no single application or initiative will make their company successful. Thus, they proceed along multiple fronts with a portfolio of projects. Some initiatives may have a greater technical focus, while others may involve more human or organizational analytical capabilities.

Know the Limits of Analytics. Good analytical leaders know when to use their intuition. They blend art and science in decision making. They use analytics whenever possible but can also see the big picture. Some aspects of business—for example, detecting major shifts in business models and customer value—require the human brain.

Case Studies of Analytical Leaders

To make these abstract attributes concrete, we present four case studies of analytical leaders at different organizational levels, each obtained through interviews with the relevant individuals. Highlighted in *italic type* are the attributes we delineated in the preceding list (just in case you've forgotten them already).

Shannon Antorcha, Analytical Department Leader,

Carnival Cruise Lines

Shannon Antorcha is a direct, enthusiastic provider of analytical database marketing capabilities at Carnival Cruise Lines, which is the flagship brand under Carnival Corporation, the world's largest cruise operator. She's been at Carnival for ten years, starting in revenue management and moving to lead the six-person database marketing function in 2006. Carnival isn't yet what we'd call an analytical competitor, but it has made enormous strides in its analytical capabilities, and Shannon has been a major contributor to the organization's progress.

Shannon has worked to *hire smart people* in her function. "Everybody has a different skill and a different set of relationships," she says. "We play good cop and bad cop with the different groups where we have strong relationships; if one member of my group has a strong relationship with, say, the IT function, she'll be the good cop, and I'll be the bad cop, always asking for more from them." She also attempts to *build an analytical ecosystem* by forming relationships with IT, other groups in the marketing function, the chief marketing officer, the CEO, and external providers of software and services such as SAS.

Her group often digs in and *sets a hands-on example* for how to use analytics. Shannon notes:

> When I joined Carnival nine years ago, it was evident to me that the organization was very operationally focused. We made many business decisions with highly tuned intuition (i.e., it just feels right given business experience) or on a cost basis (i.e., it will save money this year versus last). As one of the first members of a highly analytical revenue management start-up team, we had a daunting task ahead. A data warehouse was a relatively new concept, as were data mining, analytics, and BI. This needed to be built from the ground up, practically overnight. I have learned that individuals or business units need to accept responsibility for their deliverables. For example, being an active participant in IT projects from inception keeps the projects on time, on budget, and within scope. Our philosophy is to be involved in an IT project from the beginning. We whiteboard architecture with the IT team, while looking at table structures and doing data discovery exercises. We follow that up by being proactive through the development stage and even into system testing. Following this approach, when it comes time for the users to accept the solution that was built by IT, there are no surprises. At Carnival, I was one of the first to participate with IT in this way. In a short time, we have built a robust data warehouse and we have increased demand for analytical insight throughout the organization.

Shannon tries to *teach* other business functions about what's possible with analytics: "If you're going to be a change agent, you have to educate people and help them understand what you're trying to do. Eventually you will get their buy-in." When she came to

Carnival, Shannon says, she was impatient and less diplomatic than she is now. Over time, she has improved her *people skills* through awareness, working to improve, and coaching from mentors.

Shannon sees developing more analytical capabilities at Carnival as a long-term initiative. She has exhibited *persistence over time*: "We just keep plugging away at it—at times there is overwhelming support for our theories and ideas. At other times, we meet with resistance. I just wait it out." Her group also *works along multiple fronts*, but organizes its projects within a *strategic context*: "We juggle over a hundred different initiatives at one time. What is important is to keep a pulse on the strategic vision of our leadership team to ensure we are prioritizing these initiatives in alignment with that vision."

When asked how she measures success, Shannon describes improvements in relationships, noting, "We're no longer perceived as a weird species." A second measure is the growing demand for her group's services: "We've shown what we're capable of doing, and now there is more demand than we can address. We've got a long way to go with analytics, but we have made great progress."

Greg Poole, Business Function Leader, Talbots

Greg Poole arrived at Talbots, a leading retailer of classic women's clothing, only six months before we interviewed him. He fills the new position of executive vice president and chief supply chain officer. He had previously held supply chain roles at retailers Ann Taylor and Gap, as well as retailers in Europe.

Greg says that analytics are "part of his DNA." He likes to work from a position of fact. Talbots has not historically been very analytical in its decision making, and Greg feels that he and other members of the management team were brought into the company in part to inject a more analytical orientation. The entire leadership team is new to Talbots, and their goal is to turn around the company's performance in an extremely difficult economic climate. Greg plans to *build an analytical ecosystem*, working in particular with the new CFO, the new head of a financial planning group in the merchandising organization, and an external consultant he's using to gather and analyze data. He's also bringing key suppliers into the network by informing them of Talbots' financial position and giving them greater visibility into orders and business processes. He takes every opportunity to *teach* the rest of the organization about the analytical transformation he believes is necessary and has already presented to multiple groups around the company and to suppliers.

One of Greg's earliest moves was to *set strategy and performance expectations* with the leadership of the supply chain organization. The three-pronged strategy is to focus on product quality, improve speed to market, and improve the sourcing cost position. He defined specific numeric targets in each area, and Talbots has already achieved some of them. Each product category owner also has targets, particularly in the area of margin improvement. Greg himself has *signed up for results* by offering a margin improvement to the company's board of directors. He is *working along multiple fronts* by having analytical objectives for each strategic goal. For example, to help meet the cost position goal, he and his sourcing managers conduct "fact-based negotiation" with suppliers, improving metrics and analyses of supplier costs, relative prices paid, and price/volume curves.

Greg is continually *pushing for more data and analysis*, and is *setting a hands-on example* in doing so. One wall of his office is covered not with the usual inspirational posters and clipped *Dilbert* strips, but with charts and graphs. At each meeting of the supply chain leaders, he communicates key metrics, many of which have never been used before at Talbots. He is, however, aware that analytical progress will require *persistence over time*. At one of his previous firms, he says, it took three years to make the kind of transition he's planned for Talbots, and that firm had substantially more resources. Fortunately, he feels that there are plenty of low-hanging opportunities for improvement.

Greg clearly has strong *people skills*, and seems to *know the limits of analytics*. While he's introducing a large number of new supply chain management and analytical approaches to his organization (and to their suppliers), he is careful not to overwhelm the group or force them to use any particular approach. By setting a good example and creating a performance context, he hopes that managers and employees will see that using analytics is the only way to succeed.

Tom Anderson, Division Head and Entrepreneur

Tom Anderson is a confident executive with a straightforward manner. He's been an analytical executive at several different firms, and knows that his analytical skills are one of his key strengths as a manager and leader.

After receiving an MS in Management at MIT, Tom worked for McKinsey & Company as a consultant, primarily to the financial services industry. He says that he always sought out the most quantitative modeling–oriented client projects in that role. After becoming a partner at McKinsey he left for Capital One, the highly analytical credit card and consumer financing business, to head the young adult (customers twenty-five and younger) business unit. He explains, "Capital One appealed to me because of the 'information-based strategy' approach they take. It was a lot of nonhierarchical problem solving. Anyone could suggest new analytical approaches, regardless of their level."

Capital One had a strong testing culture, but he did not view testing as an end in itself. "If you're allowed to do whatever test you want, something is bound to stick. But in the long run that's not sustainable. Every test costs money. I felt we needed to track the impact and the rollout, and ensure that we achieved value," Anderson remembers. He constantly *pushed for data and analysis*, but he told employees, "Before you do the analysis, write the document with the charts about the results, the why, and what you would do with it."

Though Capital One had a lot of analytical people, he still had to demonstrate some of the analytical approaches he advocated. "You have to become a *teacher*," he notes. "Some people already have the problem-solving capabilities, and you have to teach them the math. Others know the math, but don't know how to apply it to business problems." At times he *set a hands-on example* by doing the analysis himself, and showing others what he had done.

The young adult business did very well under Anderson's leadership. It had historically made about $20 million in profit each year. "After about six months figuring out the business," he says, "we made $70 million the next twelve months." But Anderson wanted more autonomy, so he asked to take over a medical financing business that Capital One had acquired. He *signed up for results* with Capital One's CEO Rich Fairbank, promising to turn the business around. The medical finance business was losing millions a year; when Anderson left, it was making tens of millions a year and loan originations were up 150 percent year over year.

Tom seeks opportunities where there is no single "silver bullet," but the chance to *work along multiple fronts*. "The beauty of analytics," he suggests, "is that you find lots of things that can be incrementally improved." He *looks for leverage* where analytics can make a major difference to performance: "If it's a multiplicative business, as medical finance was, and you can improve each factor—the number of doctors times the number of patients times the percentage that seek financing—by 10 percent, it's huge."

Tom left Capital One to lead a start-up business called UPromise, in which consumers receive money toward college costs when they spend money at certain businesses. Again, he sought leverage. The business had been focused only on acquiring new members, but he extended the scope to the percentage and dollar volume of purchases by members through UPromise. Eventually UPromise was sold, and Tom had little desire to stay at the acquiring company—in part because its leaders were not analytically oriented.

In each of these businesses, Tom attempted to *hire smart people*. The key to finding good people, he believes, is the combination of analytical and *people skills*. He believes he has both, and he seeks both in those who work for him. Some of his people left the Capital One young adults unit to join him at the medical finance business. Some also left Capital One to join him at UPromise. He's still keeping track of some of them for his next venture, which will undoubtedly have an analytical orientation.

Jim and Chris McCann, CEO and President, 1-800-Flowers.com

Jim and Chris McCann are brothers who together run the 1-800-Flowers.com business. Jim is the founder, chairman, and CEO; Chris serves as president. The company originated as a single florist shop in New York and is now the world's leading florist and gift company, with more than $700 million in revenues and a database of more than 35 million customers. In addition to its 1-800-Flowers.com consumer floral business, the company has also become a leading player in the gourmet food and gift baskets category with such brands as Fannie May Confections, The Popcorn Factory, and Cheryl & Co. cookies.

Jim and Chris are both analytical leaders, but their leadership priorities and styles differ markedly. Jim notes: "Chris is much more analytical than I am. I'm ten years older than Chris, and he's learned from my mistakes. I have gotten more analytical over time, but I'm a florist and a social worker by background; neither group is known for its analytics!" Nevertheless, Jim's focus on emotion as well as analytics is a strong asset in a business built around gifting and celebratory occasions.

Chris concurs: "We have created a good working style. Jim's decision-making style is much more intuitive. I may think he's crazy with an idea, but he keeps driving it. I want to see the analytics. It helps us to avoid mistakes, but we've realized that Jim is usually right with his intuition." Chris also notes that they use data differently: "Jim's style is to gather a little bit of data, and then begin to move quickly. I'm more oriented to having greater amounts of data, and then making a commitment. But I may stick with it for too long; Jim is better at seeing trends." Clearly the two executives *know the limits of analytics* as well as those of intuition; both also have *good people skills* as well as an orientation to numbers.

The two brothers divide up strategic priorities. They have three strategic themes for the current economy: focusing on customers, reducing costs, and innovating for the future. Chris is heavily focused on the first two, which are amenable to better understanding with data and analysis. Jim is more focused on innovation, which is more intuition-friendly. Together they are clearly *setting a strategy and performance expectations* for analytical work.

Chris sees one aspect of his role as *pushing for more data and analysis*. He says, "We have a culture of analytics and testing. I say, 'I know what you think—tell me what you can prove.' We also subscribe to that comment, 'In God we trust; all others bring data.'" Jim supports these maxims, though he may come up with an initial idea through personal relationships or observations. For example, he realized that one of the company's products was perhaps too expensive when his son, a successful hedge fund employee, told him that he couldn't afford to send it very often. But before taking action, the company gathered data to support that hypothesis.

When the McCanns decide to buy a company, they view analytical skills as one of the capabilities that the parent brings to the new brand. However, they don't assume that their capabilities are always superior. Chris notes: "When we acquire a company we usually move them as quickly as possible into our analytical environment. But we bought a gift baskets company that had better merchandising and planning capabilities than we did, so we adopted many of their practices."

In addition to using analytics in their own businesses, they are *building an analytical ecosystem* in the broader floral industry. They own the BloomNet network, which sends flower orders to local florists for fulfillment. They have substantial data on what flowers are ordered under what conditions, and they are beginning to share the data and analysis with florists and even flower growers.

The brothers McCann are clearly *working along multiple fronts* with regard to analytics. They have analytical approaches to operations, finance, customer relationships, and several other aspects of the business. In marketing, they attempt to combine an intuitive understanding of customers with the data and analyses that describe them; they use "personas" to embody market research in specific hypothetical individuals. "Tina," Jim observes, "is a persona representing one of our best customers; she loves gifting, and views it as part of maintaining relationships. Having a name and a set of attributes for her is much more meaningful to our people than the demographic averages on which she is based."

They believe that *hiring smart people* with analytical skills is critical to their success. "As we look at talent now," Jim relates, "senior people must have analytical capability. They have to embrace data." Not everybody has to be purely analytical, however, as Chris notes: "We have some very creative merchants and designers who are great at what they do. We try to complement them with analytical support where needed."

It is perhaps unusual to find such complementary orientations to decision making in two brothers. But the McCanns argue that other companies can emulate their style with two executives who aren't related: "We think there should be two at the top in every company," Jim says—and Chris agrees.

Of course, the four examples of analytical leaders described in this chapter cannot represent the full range of approaches and styles. They do illustrate, however, that analytical leaders embody a variety of traits, and that analytical orientation is a critical aspect of leadership that should be more widely recognized in contemporary business.

It should also be clear from these examples that analytical leaders are not one-dimensional, numbers-obsessed cyborgs with stunted intuition. Instead, they are well-rounded individuals with both analytical and people skills. A good analytical leader is simply a good leader in general who happens to have a strong analytical orientation.

"Analytical leadership" is not a well-understood topic in the management literature, but if you speak with people at any level who are trying to make their organizations more analytical, they'll attest to its importance. What they may not realize is that analytical leadership is not just the province of the CEO and the organization's senior-most executives, but of any manager or individual contributor who seeks to make an impact.

Leadership Through the Stages

Rather than lay out a methodological approach to leadership in the chapter thus far, we've shown attributes and personalities. But next, we describe the different leadership environments as organizations move through the stages of analytical capability. A summary of these changes is given in table 4-1.

From Stage 1 to Stage 2. If your organization has analytical leaders at stage 1, they are likely to be both quite low in the leadership hierarchy and quite dissatisfied with the "analytically impaired" status of their employer. The best way to get from stage 1 to stage 2 is for leaders in business functions to emerge or be hired. They don't need to toot their analytical horns a lot, but they do need to get analytical projects going and achieve some business results, so their organization will start noticing. The projects need only to achieve significant value—no loud

TABLE 4-1

Moving to the next stage: Leadership

From stage 1 *Analytically Impaired* to stage 2 *Localized Analytics*	From stage 2 *Localized Analytics* to stage 3 *Analytical Aspirations*	From stage 3 *Analytical Aspirations* to stage 4 *Analytical Companies*	From stage 4 *Analytical Companies* to stage 5 *Analytical Competitors*
Encourage the emergence of analytical leaders in functions and business units.	Create a vision of how analytics will be used in the organization in the future, and begin to identify the specific capabilities necessary.	Engage senior leaders in building analytical capabilities, particularly in the areas of data, technology, and analytical human resources.	Encourage leaders to be very visible with their analytical capabilities, and to communicate with internal and external stakeholders about how analytics contribute to success.

huzzahs are necessary yet—so the stage will be set for the next level of leadership roles.

From Stage 2 to Stage 3. In stage 3, organizations develop analytical aspirations. How do they develop them? Through the attitudes and actions of leaders. The aspirations at this point should go beyond improving particular functions; they should aim to benefit the entire organization. Therefore, the leaders who must step up must at least control major business units, but ideally work as senior executives of the entire enterprise.

Their job is to create a vision for how analytics will transform their business in the future—perhaps not possible today, but in, say, two or four years. Leaders of a pharmaceutical or health care organization could address how their businesses will be transformed by personalized medicine. Investment firms' leaders might address how investment decision support might change their business and relationships with customers. The idea behind such a vision is that it would inspire more aggressive analytical activity and provide a conceptual umbrella for disparate projects that need to be coordinated.

From Stage 3 to Stage 4. Stage 4 is about building capability and resources—not vision, but execution; not talk, but action. Leaders at this stage are diligently working away on analytical projects and infrastructure, even though their firms may have other strategic priorities. Senior executives are insisting on fact-based and analytical decision making, and building it into the organization as one—but not necessarily the most prominent—cultural attribute.

The roles of functions that support analytics are particularly important at this stage. CIOs build the technology and data infrastructure for analytics. Line managers and human resource executives ensure that people with analytical backgrounds are hired and retained. Functional leaders, who built standalone analytical applications at earlier stages, align with other executives and create cross-functional, integrated applications. Analytical leaders at lower levels of the organization communicate and coordinate with each other, anticipating a time when analytics will become a central feature of their firms' strategies.

From Stage 4 to Stage 5.   Stage 5, with its visible-to-all analytical competition, is a "coming out party" for firms that have been at stage 4. The firm's analytical capabilities move front and center and are displayed to the world. Leaders who have quietly pursued analytical activities need to become expert communicators about their work, both internally and externally. They not only have to do great analytical work but also have to persuade customers, investors, and even the press that their analytics provide a significant advantage. And since analytical competitors can never rest, leaders at this stage need to resist complacency and static analytical tactics. Continual review of analytics and their fit to the organization is required (as we discuss in chapter 9). It takes talented leaders both to celebrate the analytical achievements of their organizations and to spur them on to further exploration and growth.

Keep in Mind . . .

- Leaders should set a good example of analytical activity themselves.
- Analytical and fact-based decisions should be rewarded, and their absence rebuked.
- Leaders must find and nurture other people and organizations who can help their firms develop analytical capabilities.

- Leaders mustn't let smart analysts snow them with analytical methods and tools that the analysts themselves can't explain in straightforward terms.

- Leaders don't rely totally on analytics in decision making; good decisions are often a mix of art and science.

- Leaders must find and nurture other people and organizations that can help their firms develop analytical capabilities.

5

TARGETS

Picking Your Spots for Analytics

EVERY BUSINESS WE KNOW can benefit from becoming more analytical across the board——in how it understands its customers, performs its operations, and makes its decisions. But even the most analytically oriented company needs to target its analytical efforts where they will do the most good, because resources, especially talent, are always constrained. And all business opportunities aren't created equal—few confer breakthroughs in performance or differentiation in the marketplace.

Of course, for companies just embarking on the analytical journey, a specific business problem may be a good initial target. Perhaps customers are complaining about service or quality, or performance benchmarks show that a business process is wasting resources, or a competitor has raised the bar and you need analytics to determine and execute a response. At Princess Cruises in 2000, for example, the initial target was revenue management. The CEO knew that other travel-oriented industries were doing this aggressively, but Princess's capability was only rudimentary, and it was easy to spot the lost revenue opportunity in every empty cabin as a ship left port.[1]

As analytical experience and success grow, targets become broader and more strategic: to optimize key business processes over time, and to innovate and operate in ways that differentiate the business in the eyes and experience of its customers. By stage 3, if they haven't done so earlier, companies should be targeting their analytical investments at their *distinctive capabilities*. These are the capabilities and integrated business processes that serve customers in ways that are differentiated from competitors and that create an organization's formula for business success and therefore offer the richest targets.[2] Princess, for example, began to focus on the analytical opportunities inherent in customer relationships—database marketing and targeted customer promotions.

A good target is so important to the business, so full of opportunity, that it engages top management commitment and creates momentum. It focuses on generating insight rather than merely information. And it is both ambitious and approachable—ambitious in that it impacts the business, and approachable in that it has access to the resources and capabilities to succeed. For example, Sir Terry Leahy (if you do well with analytics, perhaps you, too, can become a British knight), the CEO of the Europe-based grocery retailer Tesco, says that the mission of the company is to earn and grow the lifetime loyalty of its customers. Their core aim, he says, is "to understand customers better than anyone." Having more information about customers is one side of the Tesco story, but Leahy notes that information benefits customers as well: "[Access to information] helps retailers know much more about what their customers want and think. But it also gives customers a very powerful tool. They can compare prices and buy online at the click of a mouse. They can look at a retailer's ethical or environmental policies and find out what is being said about them anywhere in the world."[3] Tesco's visionary target is world-class customer knowledge.

In this chapter, we discuss two basic targeting activities: *finding your opportunities* and *setting your ambition*. We offer some tools and techniques for doing each thoroughly and well. We introduced one in chapter 1—the analytical questions matrix in figure 1-1 can help you inventory and assess your analytical *coverage* in a business domain. Another, the "ladder" of analytics applications, can help you adjust your analytical *ambition*. Using supply chain and marketing processes as examples, we demonstrate how one, or perhaps both, tools should fit your organization's style. Finally, we review how targets and the process of setting them change as a company moves along the five stages of analytical progress.

Finding Your Opportunities

Some organizations are content to take their opportunities wherever they find them. Their efforts (figure 5-1 illustrates one such effort), are often misplaced. We encourage you to be much more purposeful.

FIGURE 5-1

Alex tackles a business problem

Source: Reproduced by permission of Charles Peattie and Russell Taylor, www.alexcartoon.com.

The organization's strategic plan, which is all about finding opportunities for business growth, innovation, differentiation, and marketplace impact, seems like a logical place to look for target opportunities. But you may not find what you're looking for when you pull a page from the strategic planning binder (Okay, it's probably a PowerPoint file or a PDF by now.) It may indicate what business domain—customer service, product customization, emerging market—is important, but not what activities in that domain to target with analytics. Until the strategy formulation process incorporates an appreciation of analytics and gets specific about analytical targets (a time well beyond retirement for most of us), you may need to look in other places to discover analytical opportunities.

Most businesses also start looking for new ideas and practices by surveying what's happening elsewhere in their industries. What business and industry trends suggest the need or opportunity to change? Table 5-1 lists some of the most common applications of analytics that you're likely to find. Look across your industry—and scrutinize the activities of your competitors—on a regular basis. It keeps you alert and

TABLE 5-1

Common analytical applications

Industry	Analytical applications
Financial services	Credit scoring, fraud detection, pricing, program trading, claims analysis, underwriting, customer profitability
Retail	Promotions, replenishment, shelf management, demand forecasting, inventory replenishment, price and merchandizing optimization
Manufacturing	Supply chain optimization, demand forecasting, inventory replenishment, warranty analysis, product customization, new product development
Transportation	Scheduling, routing, yield management
Health care	Drug interaction, preliminary diagnosis, disease management
Hospitality	Pricing, customer loyalty, yield management
Energy	Trading, supply, demand forecasting, compliance
Communications	Price plan optimization, customer retention, demand forecasting, capacity planning, network optimization, customer profitability
Services	Call center staffing, service/profit chain
Government	Fraud detection, case management, crime prevention, revenue optimization
Online	Web metrics, site design, recommendations to customers
Every business	Performance management

informed about what you must do to keep pace not only with the competition, but also with changing and rising customer expectations.

Now that we've gotten you excited about this great chart, we must note that looking within your own industry will only take you so far. In fact, it can be very limiting. Your industry will tell you what it takes to maintain parity of performance, but you must be more creative to discover opportunities for differentiation. Following your industry means running with the pack, not getting out ahead. Stage 5 companies—Wal-Mart, Progressive Insurance, Marriott, Harrah's—all strive to be first to market with analytical capabilities, not just to match their industries.

That's why we recommend two additional approaches to finding analytical opportunities. Both are fundamental to understanding your business and its performance drivers, and should be exercised regularly:

- *Big-picture thinking* about the shape of your business and the trends affecting it: demographic shifts, economic trends, and changes in what customers want. This involves assessing where performance can improve and what factors drive performance. It also entails exploring your hunches about the business, what makes it tick, and where the next breakthrough may await.

- *Conducting a systematic inventory* of your key business processes, the methods for decision making within them, and the business decisions (from making an acquisition to issuing a line of credit) that could benefit from more and better analytics.

Practice Big-Picture Thinking

There are a variety of tools for big-picture thinking about your business, its performance drivers, and its opportunities for differentiation. Use the tools that your company is familiar with and that have served it well. (If we were strategy gurus, we'd be lying on the beach in the Caribbean by now.) Most of them decompose your "core processes" in some way to explore how your many activities contribute to the overall results of your business. For example, Harrah's managers knew they wanted to drive growth through customer loyalty and data-driven marketing operations—the firm's distinctive capability. They used a "service-profit chain" model to understand and target key decision areas, using clear metrics for each activity (see figure 5-2).

High-potential targets for business analytics vary by industry dynamics and, of course, by how firms add *value* in the marketplace. Companies that produce physical assets (sometimes called "value chain" firms) may want to focus on problems of supply/demand fluctuations, cost of assets, flexibility of operations, and interfaces with others in the supply chain. Pharmaceutical companies and others whose value is linked to the quality, quantity, and marketability of their intellectual property ("value shops") should concentrate on analytical experimentation and decision making. Internet businesses (like Facebook or eBay), financial institutions, telecommunications companies, and other "value network"–based firms should examine how analytics can help them increase their customer and service networks.[4]

This kind of value-based analysis can serve two important functions. First, it can help you focus on the fundamental objectives of the business and the ways analytics can serve them. A telecommunications company that pursues efficient call center utilization over customer service might save money but shoot itself in the foot by driving customers away. Second, it can suggest places to look outside your industry for

FIGURE 5-2

Harrah's analytical model

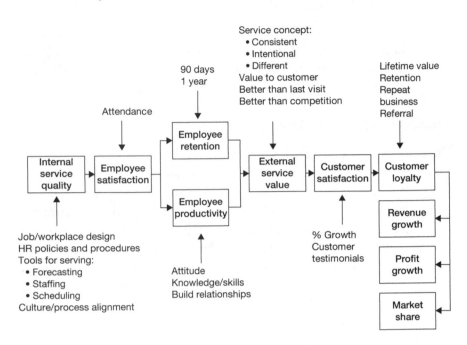

Source: James L. Heskett, Thomas O. Jones, Gary W. Loveman, W. Earl Sasser Jr., and Leonard A. Schlesinger, "Putting the Service-Profit Chain to Work," *Harvard Business Review*, March–April 1994.

fresh examples of analytical applications. When looking across industries for inspiration, your best hunting grounds are likely to be other industries with your value type (e.g., telecom companies learning from financial institutions). These are companies that face analogous business problems but in different contexts, and their analytical applications may be recognizable, relevant, and transferable.

Ironically (given our focus on being analytical), choosing your target for analytics may be based on an intuition. For example:

- Something you've always suspected about your industry but have been unable to explore or verify. What are the implicit assumptions behind how industry players operate, and which of these may be obsolete or reversible?

- Something innovative that seems logical and doable, but for which you have no evidence to prove feasible. What business problems or challenges have proven resistant to solution by other means?

- Something that you (or someone influential in the business) passionately believe is important to customers. What needs—or new forms of value—have customers themselves not yet discovered or articulated?

For example, Jim McCann, the founder and CEO of 1-800-Flowers.com, had an intuition that electronic channels were going to be important to customers wishing to order flowers and gifts. His company was the first florist on CompuServe back in 1992 and the first merchant partner of AOL. It launched a stand-alone Web site in 1995—an early Web presence for any retailer. It continues to stress search engine optimization, call center responsiveness, and early adoption of any new technology to get to customers—most recently, Twitter and an iPhone app.

Okay, but what's the analytical angle? Befitting perhaps the first company with a multichannel name, 1-800-Flowers.com has an integrated customer data warehouse and customer relationship analytics across all its brands and channels. The customer "path to purchase" is coded for all interactions, multivariate testing is done across channels, and a predicted preferred channel exists for each interaction with each customer. It easily tracks, for example, the effectiveness of online versus offline promotions.

Jim McCann has proven the potential effectiveness of the informed hunch to find new opportunities. But when using intuition, follow his brother Chris McCann's advice: verify it by gathering data and analyzing it or doing a small-scale test of the idea and expand it only if it seems to be working.

Conduct a Systematic Inventory

If the big-picture frameworks ask how the major pieces of the business fit together, a systematic inventory looks more closely at how business processes are structured and function, how decisions are made within them, and where the opportunities for dramatic improvement may be. A logical place to start: what business processes are under pressure and would benefit the most from performance breakthroughs?

Here is a quick catalog of the kinds of business processes that lend themselves to analytics:

- *Data-rich.* Analytics unleash the potential of the data you've got.

- *Information-intensive.* Analytics reveal the meaning of data.

- *Asset-intensive.* Analytics enable effective utilization and sharing of scarce or expensive resources.

- *Labor-intensive.* Analytics enable decision making and the leverage of expertise, especially where talent supply is short, talent demand is cyclical, and training times are lengthy.

- *Dependent on speed and timing.* Analytics enable process acceleration and real-time decisions, especially where customer satisfaction or process competitiveness demand superhuman response times (e.g., via the Web).

- *Dependent on consistency and control.* Analytics enable consistent decisions even in unpredictable cases.

- *Dependent on distributed decision making.* Analytics enable decision makers to look upstream and downstream to anticipate the effects of their actions.

- *Cross-functional or cross-business in scope.* Analytics reveal interdependencies and enable the parts to work together better.

- *Low average success rate.* Processes with a low "batting average" are probably ripe for improvement through analytics.

For example, McKesson Pharmaceutical targeted its complex supply chain. The company has one of the highest-volume distribution networks in the world, routing one-third of the medicines consumed in the U.S. market to more than twenty-five thousand locations a day. With major pharmaceutical manufacturers on the supply side and powerful retailers (including Wal-Mart) on the customer side, McKesson has to operate at high volume and high efficiency. Building on its strong process orientation, the company brought together data from the sales, logistics, purchasing, and finance processes to achieve more integrated analysis and decision support. Now managers throughout the supply chain can look all the way up and downstream to evaluate the operational and financial impact of their decisions regarding delivery schedules, transportation utilization, quantity adjustments, product dating, and drop shipping.

You can also find analytical opportunities by assessing your business decisions (regardless of their association with well-defined business processes) and asking how better information and analysis might yield better results. In general, look for the following six conditions: (1) complex decisions with lots of variables and steps; (2) simple decisions in which consistency is either desirable or required by law (like nondiscriminatory credit and lending); (3) places where you need to optimize the process or activity as a whole (especially when decomposing and optimizing locally cause you to suboptimize the whole); (4) decisions in which you need to understand connections, correlations, and their significance (as in McKesson's supply chain); (5) places where you need better forecasts, anticipation, or downstream visibility (McKesson again); (6) current low average of success.

To search for targets systematically, supply chain managers and information management people can take an inventory of supply chain reporting and analytics. This will show where your efforts are concentrated and where you could be doing more. Figure 5-3 illustrates some

FIGURE 5-3

Analytical questions: Supply chain examples

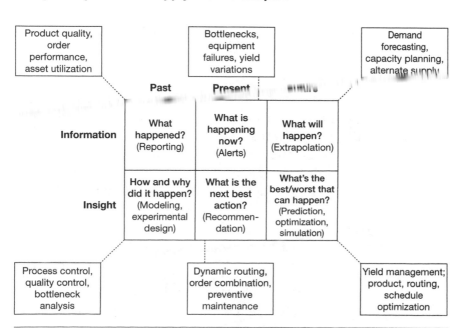

common examples for supply chain processes using the analytical questions matrix from figure 1-1. In the "information" row, conventional reporting usually centers on things like order fulfillment and asset utilization performance. Can your reports and models focused on the past be augmented to become more predictive? Can your forecasts incorporate more current and external data—and rely less on simple extrapolations from the past?

Alerts signal when bottlenecks are forming or quality is straying out of range. Extrapolating from historical trends is the first step toward modeling. Extrapolation lets you begin to anticipate future supply and demand. In the "insight" row, modeling reveals the causes of problems, so you may improve process and quality control. Real-time recommendations enable immediate responses: for example, trucks may need to take alternative routes or machines may be taken offline for emergency maintenance. And prediction, simulation, and optimization facilitate more dynamic scheduling and more precise product mix and yield management.

Establishing Your Ambition

If you've done some big-picture thinking and taken a systematic inventory of even one business domain, chances are you've got plenty of candidates for improvement through analytics. How then to prioritize, to zero in on your best targets? By carefully calibrating both your expected benefits and your available capability:

- *Benefits.* Is the business process a strategic or otherwise high priority? How big a difference might the analytical application make in business performance? Will excelling at the process yield marketplace advantage, such as setting a difficult-to-match performance standard or building a differentiated capability? Is the process high-volume enough to generate significant cost savings from speeding decisions, eliminating steps, or selecting the best process variation? If the business potential is large enough to pursue, what level of effort and investment does it warrant? And how fast must you act to realize the benefits?

- *Capabilities.* Are the necessary pieces in place—especially if the application is new? If you do lack ingredients, is there a way to buy, rent, or build them in time? Keep in mind that the five

DELTA elements are all interrelated, but targets may be the most dependent variable. They may need to be adjusted based on the availability of data and skilled analysts, the scope of an enterprise perspective, and the commitment of enterprise and business unit leadership.

We find it instructive to visualize potential ambitions on a "ladder" of analytical applications as shown in figure 5-4. Going up the ladder entails more sophisticated analytics, so the higher rungs are less populated. Skipping rungs, like on any ladder, can lead to nasty falls. Starting at the bottom rung:

- The foundation is good *data*—it is accurate, consistent, integrated, accessible, and relevant.

- Statistical analysis of that data yields useful *segmentation*—of customers, products, and transactions or other business events.

- Segmentation in turn enables *differentiated action*—treating individual customers differently, or choosing the most efficient path in a flexible business process.

FIGURE 5-4

Ladder of analytical applications

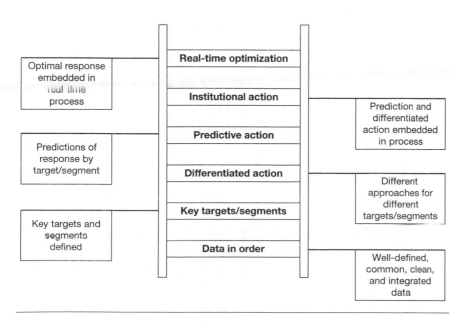

- Incorporating *predictive action* enables a business to marshal its resources where opportunity is greatest.

- At the *institutional action* rung, differentiation and prediction are embedded in ongoing business processes and accomplished automatically.

- The top rung is the domain of *real-time optimization*, where the process adjusts on the fly to maintain optimal business yield. And yes, unlike most ladders, this is one ladder where you *can* stand on the top rung.

The ladder in figure 5-4 is the general pattern. Within any major business process area, it's enlightening to ask: How high have we climbed? How high can we climb? How high does the market want us to climb? Have we compromised our performance by skipping or only partially covering a rung? And can we boost performance or gain advantage by moving up a rung? As you move up the ladder, the rungs below you will still need attention. For example, if your company acquires a competitor or if a third-party data feed changes, you need to make adjustments to keep your data in order. So maintain your perspective by keeping the entire ladder—what you've accomplished and what opportunities remain—in mind.

Of course, every business process will have its own ladder, one that reflects industry practices and standard process characteristics. For example, figure 5-5 depicts the ladder for supply chain, starting at the bottom with information about products, their sources, and what happens to them. At the second rung products are meaningfully grouped, often in terms of cost, availability from suppliers, or customers. At the third rung products are processed or priced differently, based on customer and market information. The fourth rung is more predictive, tackling the challenge of "replenishment" in a broad sense—what amount of goods and resources should you keep in the pipeline to fill anticipated orders? On the fifth rung you customize efficiently to create variety in products and processes. The top rung is the realm of real-time optimization of product flow and yield that maximizes profit.

Figure 5-6 depicts a ladder for applications of marketing analytics. At the first rung is the development of an integrated and high-quality customer database, starting with an agreed-upon definition of what constitutes a customer. Segmentation, at the second rung, is not just

FIGURE 5-5

Ladder of analytical applications: Supply chain

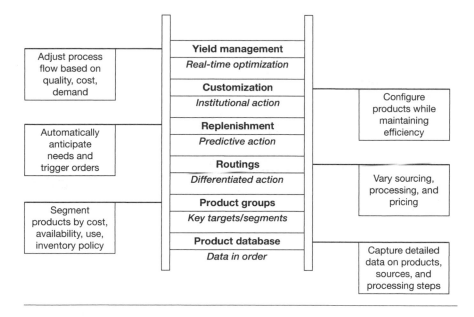

a categorization scheme, but should be the basis for treating customers differently and targeting the most valuable ones. For example, high spenders at a casino may be offered a complimentary upgrade or dinner upon check-in, or digital camera buyers can receive a coupon for a new printer four weeks after initial purchase. At the third rung a business process can trigger immediate actions in response to a customer's activity. For example, banks might send a simple "thank-you" or confirmation e-mail after an online transaction, or a call after a large deposit is made into a checking account. The fourth rung represents overall campaign management and personalization—for example, tracking which customers received which offers and how they responded. At the fifth rung predictive analytics help forecast how customers will behave in the future and predict which offers will conclude in a sale. One insurance company used predictive analytics to cut direct marketing volume by 50 percent while doubling revenue. Finally, at the top rung of the ladder is the ability for a company to make a real-time offer to a customer with a high probability of acceptance. For example, if an online travel booking site sees a customer search for flights but then

FIGURE 5-6

Ladder of analytical applications: Marketing

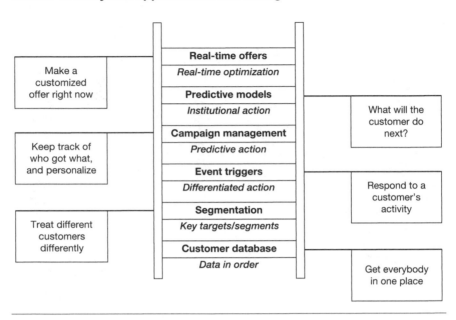

log off without purchasing, the site could immediately send the customer an e-mail offering a reduced price or a hotel or rental car for that trip.

We recommend developing ladders for every major business process area, including internal processes like employee management, finance, and overall business performance management. They will help you see both how far you've come analytically and where you can aspire to go next.

Be warned that the targeting methods we've discussed won't yield a scoped and specified project, complete with resource plan, timetable, and metrics. You've got more work to do at that level. Chances are, your targeting will trigger commitment to a pilot or experiment that can enable you to further refine the target. And even after a major analytics project is under way, you'll want to revisit these targeting questions (see "Do We Have a Good Target?") periodically and adjust accordingly. As your organization grows more analytical, targeting becomes a continuous exercise—seeking additional opportunities in areas where you're already applying analytics, as well as keeping an eye out for opportunities not yet conceived.

Do We Have a Good Target?

- Is it aimed at a distinctive capability, an area that can make a difference in business performance, competitiveness, and profitability?

- Are executive management and relevant business area managers behind the initiative?

- Does it contain elements of innovation and differentiation (e.g., by bringing together information and capabilities from adjoining parts of the business)?

- Does it have specific goals and metrics, including ways to gauge both progress and eventual success?

- Is it feasible given the availability of resources and capabilities (including the other DELTA elements)?

Targets Through the Stages

How does targeting happen at the most analytically advanced, stage 5 companies? The company targets analytics where it has the greatest effect on business performance and differentiation. Ambitions are clear, and analytical projects enjoy the momentum that comes with compelling business rationale and specific strategic objectives. At any given time the company is probably working on one major, competitively differentiating target and perhaps several minor ones. Once it reaches a major goal, it moves on to another one—while maintaining its edge in the first. And the analytical techniques employed successfully are translated quickly to targets in other parts of the business. For example, Google was founded on analytics about page rank and search. It later moved on to analytics about which ads to display under what circumstances. The company continually researches and innovates around both targets.

The methods of targeting are very sophisticated at stage 5. The company always has its eyes and ears—both human and electronic—alert to changing times, new ways to differentiate, and tomorrow's targets. It taps all sources of insight into potential targets—both big-picture thinking about the structure and purpose of the business (based on industry trends

TABLE 5-2

Moving to the next stage: Targets

From stage 1 Analytically Impaired to stage 2 Localized Analytics	From stage 2 Localized Analytics to stage 3 Analytical Aspirations	From stage 3 Analytical Aspirations to stage 4 Analytical Companies	From stage 4 Analytical Companies to stage 5 Analytical Competitors
Work wherever there is sponsorship and some decent data. Target "low-hanging fruit."	Work with business areas that are already somewhat analytical or can benefit greatly from analytics. Target business process or cross-functional applications. Start taking systematic inventories of analytical opportunities by business area.	Work with major business processes and their owners. Focus on high value and high impact targets. Take an enterprisewide approach to finding and evaluating targets. Formalize the process of targeting as a collaboration among business executives, IT and analytics leaders.	Work with the executive team. Focus on strategic initiatives, value creation, and building distinctive capability that will enhance competitive differentiation. Infiltrate the strategic planning process so analytics can shape (not just respond to) business strategy.

and market demand) and systematic inventory of business processes and decisions. Perhaps most important, at stage 5 there is an enterprisewide perspective (the *E* of DELTA) on the evaluation and pursuit of analytical opportunities—those targets that can make the most difference in overall business performance.

Table 5-2 summarizes what it takes to advance from stage to stage in terms of targeting.

From Stage 1 to Stage 2. At stage 1, you're starting from scratch, and you are largely targetless. To progress to stage 2, you've got to generate interest and show some early success. Start with a business manager who has a problem and some decent data for addressing it. If you start with good data that requires minimal cleanup before analysis, you avoid delay the first time out of the box. It's also best to show success early, so the first targets should be "low-hanging fruit"—business problems and objectives that are clear, definitely worthwhile, and doable fairly quickly. Once you've established a bit of a track record, your ambition and degree of difficulty can rise.

From Stage 2 to Stage 3. The first few projects may be opportunistically selected, but after a few successes you should enlist business sponsors who are interested in taking systematic inventory of analytical opportunities in their process or decision areas. Once you've reached stage 2, there may a veritable shooting gallery of targets in play, but few if any of high business importance because they are too local. To move to stage 3, you need to focus on important targets and raise your ambition in those areas. Targets become cross-functional, involving more businesspeople in analytics projects, thus necessitating a more collaborative targeting process. Now is a good time to introduce some big-picture thinking about analytical opportunities and business impact, and to encourage an enterprisewide perspective in targeting.

From Stage 3 to Stage 4. At stage 3, your analytical targets are important, but are you pursuing the *most* important ones? To move to stage 4, you need to formalize the methods of finding high-impact business opportunities, evaluate them from an enterprise viewpoint, and fund them with adequate money and resources. In a decentralized company that has analytical opportunities spanning the business units, establish a small "program management office" to coordinate analytical projects and their resourcing. Get senior executives across the enterprise not just involved in, but supportive of the methods the company uses to deploy analytics.

From Stage 4 to Stage 5. Congratulations! You've reached stage 4. Analytics is now a regular part of how the company works. The final step is to put analytics to work strategically where it adds greatest value for your customers and differentiates you from your competitors. To put it another way, make your organization's analytical capabilities and expertise an essential part of how you go to market. Now you've got to be working with the CEO and executive team, as well as analytical leaders across the enterprise. Analytical thinking and opportunity finding are embedded in the strategic planning process, and targeting analytical applications is no different from targeting any strategic business initiative. In fact, analytics are part of *any* strategic business initiative.

Keep in Mind . . .

- Look beyond what's happening in your industry. Better to differentiate than just run with the pack.

- Qualify your targets based not only on business potential, but also on whether necessary resources—starting with data—are available.

- Think ahead. Anticipate how your analytical capability will advance as you "move up the ladder" in a target business area.

- Be willing to experiment to discover what's possible.

- Don't spread your analytical efforts too thin across too many targets. Especially while the organization is still learning, focus on one major target and perhaps a few minor ones.

- Don't ignore your hunches about analytical opportunities. Just be sure to test them!

6

ANALYSTS

Managing Scarce and Valuable Talent

THOUGH COMPUTERS AND DATA drive analytical decision making, they are not nearly as vital as people; we've never seen an analytically oriented firm without plenty of analytically oriented people. Finding, developing, managing, and deploying analysts—the people who make the day-to-day-work of such organizations possible—is critical to a firm's success.

Defining Analysts

In a large corporation, hundreds or perhaps thousands of employees have the word *analyst* in their functional titles, referring broadly to anyone who uses data or information. For our purpose in this book, we define *analysts* as workers who use statistics, rigorous quantitative or qualitative analysis, and information modeling techniques to shape and make business decisions—still a broad range of activity. To fully describe the challenges of managing analytical talent, we need to distinguish four types of analytical people.[1]

Analytical Champions

These champions aren't the kind you'd see in a Gatorade commercial; they are *executive decision makers* who depend heavily on data analyses to make business decisions and who lead major analytical initiatives.

Champions are the leading advocates on how analytical techniques and technologies can be used to guide decision making. For example, Tom Anderson of Capital One and then UPromise, profiled in chapter 4, falls into this category. Analytical champions have both strong business acumen and an appreciation of analytical techniques. They communicate well about analyses because they can articulate how analytics will benefit the organization. Often analytical professionals who have been promoted into senior management, such champions establish long-term strategies and specify how to achieve them. Their expertise lies in their understanding of the business and of how analytical techniques and technologies, such as trending, forecasting, and predictive modeling, and enterprise applications systems such as SAP or Oracle, can help achieve business objectives. They often provide guidance to others in their organization on IT systems or process-related topics.

PORTRAIT OF AN ANALYTICAL CHAMPION

Steven Udvarhelyi, MD, Senior Vice President and

Chief Medical Officer, Independence Blue Cross

and Its Affiliates

Steve Udvarhelyi has overall responsibility for medical management programs and policies, provider contracting and relations, pharmacy services, and informatics at Independence Blue Cross (IBC). In overseeing informatics, Steve is responsible for corporatewide information management and reporting activities.

Analytics come naturally to Steve: "I've been a math- and science-oriented person my whole life. I like working through analytical problems." He sees his role as that of an executive advocate for implementing analytics across the enterprise. He argues passionately for the value of analytical capabilities yet recognizes that "having analytical capabilities and the best data in the world doesn't create competitive advantage. Changing the way the business uses it is the only way to create advantage."

Steve considers the attributes of a good analytical champion to be less about having the technical skills of a professional, and more about having an appreciation for the data. Most important, he says, a good analytical champion can translate the benefits of enterprisewide analytics to businesspeople in order to promote cultural and organizational change.[2]

Analytical Professionals

In the second category are the analytical professionals, the most proficient and knowledgeable employees across the range of quantitative skills. Analytical pros *create advanced analytical applications* by developing statistical models and algorithms to be used by others in the organization. Professionals typically employ advanced techniques such as trend analysis, classification algorithms, predictive modeling, statistical modeling, and optimization and simulation, as well as a variety of data-, Web-, and text-mining techniques.

Occupying the most creative level in the analytical cadre, professionals, like champions, provide analytical guidance to others in their organization. They are often involved in establishing long-term goals, specifying the best strategies to achieve them, and estimating the resources needed to accomplish them. Needless to say, you don't become an analytical professional by reading *Statistics for Dummies*. Typically, these jobs require an advanced degree (often a PhD) in a quantitative field such as economics, statistics, operations research, or mathematics, or a specialty degree in a field like biostatistics, informatics, genetics, or applied physics. For example, health insurer HCSC's special investigations department (which creates analytical solutions to detect fraud and does other specialized analytics) was led by Kyle Cheek, a PhD in political economy whose team included expertise in statistics, epidemiology, bioengineering, and business.

Professionals often have advanced technical skills, including coding in C++, SQL, and SAS.[3] The best professional analysts are not only technical and quantitative, but also skilled at explaining analytical problems and results in clear and nontechnical language. However, such a combination is difficult to find, and as we later argue, many professional analysts need translators to deal with mere businesspeople. Others in the business may view them with a mixture of awe and derision, referring to them as über-analysts, super-quants, or brainiacs. They typically make up only 5 to 10 percent of a company's analyst cadre.

Portrait of an Analytical Professional

Daryl Wansink, Director of Research and Evaluation,

Clinical Informatics Department, Blue Cross and

Blue Shield of North Carolina

With a PhD in social psychology from the University of Buffalo, Daryl Wansink originally planned on an academic research career: "But once I saw the incredible data that I would have access to [by working for a managed care provider] . . . Data is a statistician's crack and I was hooked." At Blue Cross and Blue Shield of North Carolina, Daryl is responsible for a team of analytical professionals applying statistical and experimental methods to improve health care delivery and business decisions. His biggest challenge is "to get good data from the real world that leads to definitive answers." With more than twelve years of experience, Daryl now has other analytical professionals working for him. But he still actively builds models himself (using SAS, SPSS, S-Plus, and Spotfire) because, as he says, "You have to be touching the data to understand what is going on. It is hard to delegate without getting into the model building."

As much as analytical professionals relish digging into the data, Daryl is quick to point out that "all that data is a double-edged sword. Successful analytical professionals have to have an element of pragmatism. Otherwise, you can get lost in the data for months and years and never find anything of value for the business."[4]

Analytical Semiprofessionals

The analysts in our third category *apply the models and algorithms* developed by professionals on behalf of the rest of the business. The majority of financial and marketing analysts are semipros. They may be sophisticated quants in their own right and may develop straightforward applications on occasion, but their primary role is to apply analytics to business problems for routine or specialized decision making. They are experts in data creation, collection, interpretation, and use—and in understanding the workings of a business through the structure and flow of its information. They perform complex queries and run models on data, link the analyses and insights to business results, and prepare business reports based on these analyses. Semipros are adept at working with analytical applications, visual tools for information analysis, and "what-if" tools, including marketing workbenches, financial planning models, pricing models, and sales forecasting models; statistical software, such as SAS or SPSS; and enterprise systems like SAP.

It's particularly important for semipros to be able to translate the benefits of analytics into lay language for businesspeople—for example, by bridging the gap between hard-core analytical professionals and business managers. Some semipros are primarily business analysts—often MBAs with quantitative orientations. They are often process oriented and certified in process improvement methods, such as Six Sigma. Others are primarily information and decision analysts, usually with advanced degrees in computer science. Semipros may make up 15 to 20 percent of the total analyst cadre.

PORTRAIT OF AN ANALYTICAL SEMIPROFESSIONAL

David Scamehorn, Director of Customer Behavior Analytics,

Best Buy

Dave Scamehorn has a long-standing interest in the application of mathematics to business. As an undergraduate at Macalister College, he majored in math, then earned a master's degree in statistics from the University of Minnesota. After an eight-year stint at Xcel Energy (a Minneapolis-based utility company), he was ready for a new industry and a new challenge. Dave joined Best Buy as a model builder and (if necessary) could still operate as an analytical pro. But his mission now is leading a broad customer analytics team of forty people, only fourteen of whom are full-time employees in his group. Their scope includes database strategy, tool selection and implementation, analytic consulting to the retail business, research and development of new analytic approaches, customer segmentation, and customer performance scorecard development.

While Dave has a few analytical pros working for him, most are semipros who rely on data visualization tools. These semipros work with the rest of the merchant organization to interpret and apply insights about their customers to improve business performance. His efforts have had a significant payoff. Best Buy's pricing and assortment decisions for the Christmas holiday season incorporated customer analytics for the first time in 2008, significantly improving profits from Black Friday weekend (the weekend after U.S. Thanksgiving), a remarkable achievement in one of the most dismal Christmas shopping seasons in retail history.

Dave may no longer build models at work, but he still remains an analyst at heart. "I like to keep my hands on the data. I don't get a chance to do it at work anymore, but I tinker on it at home. Strategy optimization is something I still pursue as a hobby."[5]

Analytical Amateurs

In the fourth category are the analytical amateurs, employees whose primary job is not analytical work, but who need some understanding of analytics to do their jobs successfully. By calling them "amateurs," we don't mean to be the least bit pejorative. On the contrary, amateurs are *knowledgeable consumers of analytics* who can apply analytical insights to their work. An amateur might be a business manager using data-driven insights to increase sales volume, a call center employee who relies on a "next best offer" recommendation in order to serve a customer effectively, or a warehouse manager who follows data-based advice about optimal inventory levels. Typically businesspeople who can enter and manipulate data using Excel spreadsheets and other basic information management tools, amateurs put the output of analytical models to work. They also summarize and report data to others in their organization. They include many of the most influential employees and executives in the business, people who combine information modeled by the professionals with their local data, knowledge, and experience to make analytics-based business decisions. Amateurs typically make up 70 to 80 percent (or more) of an organization's analytical talent. To illustrate their range, we profile two very different analytical amateurs.

PORTRAIT OF AN ANALYTICAL AMATEUR

Will Smith, actor

Hollywood movie star Will Smith proves that an analytical amateur doesn't have to employ complicated math to be successful. An unconventional amateur, Smith has a remarkable track record. He was voted the top money-making movie star of 2008 by theater owners and film buyers.[6] And with good reason: except for the Harry Potter series, movies featuring him have higher opening weekends and average box office receipts than those with any other male lead.[7] How did he do it? By listening to the data. *USA Today* describes him this way:

> For all the on-screen charisma that has made him a Hollywood ATM, Smith is, at his core, a statistician with social skills . . . Most Mondays, he pores over box office reports the way sports nuts read box scores . . . "I think of the universe as this big, master computer," he says. "The keyboard is inside each of us. I have a keyboard inside of me. I just have to figure out what to type, learn the code, to make the things happen that I want."[8]

Smith frequently calls himself a "student of universal patterns." When he first decided to make films, he and his business manager studied the ten top-grossing films of all time and said, "O.K., what are the patterns? We quickly realized that 10 out of 10 had special effects, 9 of 10 had special effects with creatures, and 8 of 10 had special effects with creatures and a love story."[9] This straightforward, analytically based insight didn't take a lot of effort, but it certainly made it a lot easier to choose his next two films, *Independence Day* and *Men in Black*, which were huge international hits.

Smith doesn't rely exclusively on math to choose scripts, of course. But regardless of the film's appeal to him as an artist, he always analyzes data to make his movies as successful as possible. He says one key to his success is realizing that "movie stars are not made in America. Movie stars are made when you can pull $20 million out of Brazil, or when you can do $48 million in Japan."[10] The data convinced him to travel extensively to promote his films internationally. As a result, the recent *Seven Pounds*, a movie with limited appeal in the United States, generated over $168 million gross worldwide box office sales—largely through Smith's insistence on marketing the film to an international audience.

Portrait of an Analytical Amateur

Byrne Doyle, District Manager, Best Buy Michigan

As district manager for Best Buy in Michigan, Byrne Doyle transformed one of the worst-performing districts in the company into a top performer. His colleagues credit his leadership, deep customer knowledge, analytically based insights, and willingness to teach others how analytics can improve business performance.

Byrne has filled many previous roles at Best Buy, working in operations, in customer service, and as regional finance director. This diverse background enables him to view data from multiple business perspectives and is, he says, "a tremendous advantage to how I apply analytics." A quick study who is largely self-taught, Byrne approached each new position as a way to sharpen his business acumen. Although he took some MBA courses to build his functional expertise, he describes himself as "a computer guy and a tinkerer at heart" who learned about technology, business, and statistical analysis largely by doing.

Byrne's naturally competitive nature and desire to understand the root causes of things led him to develop his skills as an analytical amateur. "The foundation of my career is that I am able make connections that other people don't make. I try not to box myself into or anticipate solutions. My first tendency is to go straight to the root cause, find the patterns that other people overlook and work back from there."

Byrne does a great job at balancing short-term (P&L/financial metrics) with longer-term customer and employee metrics. The key to using analytics from his perspective is to "distill the data down to its essence for my team. Others tend to share too much information. In our business, it comes down to some simple nuggets, like 'Grow market share and we can outperform the economy.'"

Byrne mentors his subordinates so they learn to think analytically about the business. He wants his store managers and sales associates to be proactive about how their actions can build the business rather than to react to the "metric of the month." By focusing on this single goal, he led his stores to win the employee experience award two years ago and the customer experience award last year.[11]

Analytical Skills

Quantitative skills are the core requirement for any type of analyst. But tuning a regression equation or manipulating a spreadsheet is only the beginning. Effective analysts need to be proficient not only with data, but also with people.

- *Quantitative and technical skills* are the foundation. Naturally, analytical professionals have more quantitative expertise than semipros, champions, and amateurs, but all analytical people must be proficient in the quantitative disciplines specific to their industry or business function: stochastic volatility analysis in finance, biometrics in pharmaceutical, and informatics in health care firms, for example. Analytical people must also know how to use the software tools associated with their type of analytical work, whether it be to build algorithmic models, define decision-making rules, conduct "what-if" analyses, or interpret a business dashboard.

- *Business knowledge and design skills* enable analysts to be more than simple backroom statisticians. They must be familiar with the business disciplines and processes to which analytics are being applied. They need enough general business background to work at the interfaces of business processes and problems. They also must have insight into the key opportunities and challenges facing the company, and know how analytics can be used to drive business value.[12]

- *Relationship and consulting skills* enable analysts to work effectively with their business counterparts to conceive, specify, pilot, and implement analytical applications. Relationship skills—advising, negotiating, and managing expectations—are vital to the success of all analytical projects. Furthermore, an analyst needs to communicate the results of analytical work: either within the business to share best practices and to emphasize the value of analytical projects; or outside the business, to shape working relationships with customers and suppliers, or to explain the role of analytics in meeting regulatory requirements (e.g., utility company rate cases). For this reason, we'd modify Warren Buffett's admonition from "beware of geeks bearing formulas" to "beware of geeks who can't explain the benefits and limitations of their formulas" (though that may be a large proportion of geeks, admittedly).[13]

- *Coaching and staff development skills* are essential to an analytical organization, particularly when a company has a large or fast-growing pool of analysts, or when its analytical talent is spread across business units and geographies. When analytical talent isn't centralized, coaching can ensure that best practices are shared across the company. Good coaching not only builds quantitative skills, but also helps people understand how data-driven insights can drive business value.

In practice, we've found that few individuals come equipped with the full spectrum of skills we've listed (see "About the Analytical Talent Research" for the methods we used); analytical capacity is, apparently, not yet a Darwinian evolutionary priority. Therefore, a company needs the right mix of analytical talent in its ranks of analysts. For example, you must balance pros—who focus on more advanced analytical techniques—with semipros—who have a broader skill set, combining strong analytics with business design and management skills to link professionals to their customers. Figure 6-1 shows the relative strengths of each type of analyst across the major skill categories.

FIGURE 6-1

Typical skill proficiency levels by type of analyst

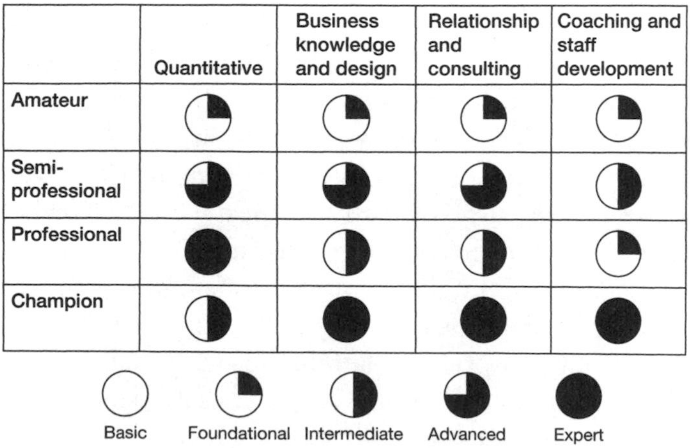

Source: Jeanne G. Harris, Elizabeth Craig, and Henry Egan, "How to Create a Talent-Powered Analytical Organization," research report, Accenture Institute for High Performance, 2009.

About the Analytical Talent Research

In 2008, the Accenture Institute for High Performance conducted a research study, "Talent Engagement, Attitudes and Motivations," to investigate what influences engagement for employees in general and for "analytical talent" in particular. A comprehensive, Web-based survey measured the personal engagement, work attitudes, and career motivations of full-time employees in a wide range of jobs and organizations. The 1,367 respondents (including 799 analysts) were U.S. employees at companies with at least $50 million in annual revenues. They represented a wide variety of industries and worked across a range of functional areas, including finance, IT, operations and production, R&D, marketing and sales, illustrated in the following figure.

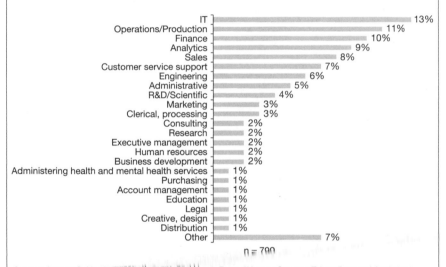

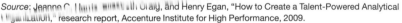

Source: Jeanne C. Harris, Elizabeth Craig, and Henry Egan, "How to Create a Talent-Powered Analytical Organization," research report, Accenture Institute for High Performance, 2009.

The good news is that our research found that analysts overall are significantly more engaged at work, more satisfied with their jobs, and more committed to their organizations than other types of employees. (The following table contains illustrations of engagement expressed by analytical versus nonanalytical talent in terms of engagement, job satisfaction and organizational commitment.)

Analytical work may seem deadly dull to the nonquants among us. But it actually has many of the attributes that lead to motivating and engaging work. Analytics require the use of a diverse mix of skills (quantitative, technical, and interpersonal), provide the opportunity to complete an entire piece of work, have a significant impact on others, allow some degree of autonomy in performing the work, and offer automatic feedback on work performance. Indeed, the analysts we surveyed reported significantly higher levels of all of these factors than did other employees, suggesting that if Karl Marx had foreseen the rise of analytics he might have been more optimistic in his theories and a generally happier person.

Differences between analysts and non-analysts

	Analysts	Non-analysts
Feel like going to work when I get up in the morning	68%	52%
Willing to really push myself to reach challenging work goals	82	66
Ready to put my heart and soul into my work	77	64
Get excited thinking about new ways to do my job more effectively	67	50
Like working at my company	78	65
Really care about the fate of my company	74	59
Willing to put in a great deal of effort beyond that normally expected in order to help my company be successful	70	51

Source: Jeanne G. Harris, Elizabeth Craig, and Henry Egan, "How to Engage and Retain Your Analytical Talent," research report, Accenture Institute for High Performance, 2009.

Motivating Analysts

Securing the analytics skills you need isn't simply a matter of getting HR to hire more quantitative experts. To find and keep analysts, you need an understanding of how they tick and an informed approach to managing them. First and foremost, analysts are motivated by *interesting and challenging work* that allows them to utilize their highly specialized skills. Challenge and complexity are essential for pros and semipros, particularly running sophisticated data analyses and developing new models and techniques. Like most analysts, Sharon Frazee, Vice President of Corporate Healthcare Analytics and Research at Walgreens, values the opportunity to do interesting work: "Money's nice, but I get more excited about doing things that are interesting, not doing the same thing every day, and having opportunities for growth—to stretch my skills."[14] Managers must be mindful of this fact as they design and organize their analyst roles. Perhaps the biggest demotivator for analytical pros is spending too much time on simple analyses and report generation instead of building and refining analytical models. We know of several organizations that have lost analysts who felt they were treated largely as "spreadsheet developers."

Variety in their work and a *sense of personal progress* keep analysts interested and challenged. One grocery retailer found it could attract highly skilled MBAs to an essential but repetitive analytic and reporting job, but could not keep them for long before they became restless and sought out new challenges. Variety comes from fresh assignments and projects, "moving around" the business to expose analysts to strategic problems and priorities, and offering blocks of time for learning and experimentation. For small analyst groups or those without precedent for analyst career paths, the chance to develop new expertise is crucial: developing new knowledge of business functions, quantitative models, analytic techniques, and software packages are just few examples of such opportunities.

Analysts also want to *do important work that makes a meaningful contribution.* The models and applications they build must matter to the business. As Sharon Frazee told us: "I want the stuff I do to make a difference . . . Being able to do the kind of informatics work that actually gets applied, and to see things changed because of it, is a lot more important to me than a lot of other stuff." Another big demotivator is feeling that only a fraction of one's work is actually used. And if the business is not demanding important analytics work, the best analysts sense that it's time to move on.

Analysts want to feel supported and valued by their organizations, but they also want *autonomy* at work—the freedom and flexibility to decide how their jobs are done. Managers should provide goals and resources, and then give analytical people freedom to organize their own work. Autonomy is not abandonment, however. Managers (and customers for that matter) need to recognize analysts' work and make their contributions visible to senior management.

In addition to thinking about *what* analysts do, it is important to consider with *whom* they work. Analysts like to be surrounded by other *smart and capable colleagues*. Grouping analysts together—whether physically in functional groups, or virtually in communities of interest—keeps them motivated. It also promotes sharing of best practices, leading to knowledge spillovers, and allows companies to tailor career models and training opportunities to better suit the needs of their analysts.

Companies that can offer analysts the chance to work with other smart analysts and businesspeople have little trouble attracting analytical talent. Steve Udvarhelyi at Independence Blue Cross reports that their informatics organization offers just such an appealing environment that helps to attract analytical talent: "It's a defined center of excellence. It creates a fertile ground for people to work with other people. It creates a critical mass where you get career opportunities, growth opportunities, and a good professional interaction."

Designing meaningful jobs and ensuring opportunities for intellectual stimulation and career growth is only half the challenge. Our research points to several other factors important for organizations to hold on to their analysts. In particular, analytical people seek a strong culture of trust—where they feel like they are treated in a fair, consistent and predictable fashion, and where they believe that the other people in the organization are open and honest and act with integrity. Positive relationships with their immediate supervisors are also particularly important to analysts (especially semipros)—even more than they are to other employees. The absence of any one of these factors will often cause analysts to head for the exits.

Organizing Analysts

One of the most common questions we hear is, "What's the best way to organize analysts?" When just getting started with analytics, it is easy enough to stash a handful of analysts in a functional department. But deciding how to organize and manage analysts (especially the highly skilled pros and semipros) becomes a management concern once executives begin to take analytics seriously. Because top analysts are a scarce and potentially very valuable resource, naturally you want to maximize their value to the business. It's wasteful to have them locked up in one part of the enterprise working on low-value projects when there is high-value work elsewhere. It's also wasteful to have them scattered across the enterprise working on small local problems and unable to band together in "critical mass" to tackle strategic initiatives. Organizational structure matters because it affects how you:

- *Deploy* people on the most important and value-adding work of the enterprise.

- *Develop* skills and experience that analysts need to maximize their potential.

For analytical professionals and semiprofessionals, organizational design boils down to two big questions (your analytical amateurs are by definition distributed across the enterprise):

- *What's the best way to group people* to align them with business units for geographical and administrative convenience and to enable them to work with and learn from each other regularly?

- *What are the best ways to coordinate* among groups to impart an enterprise perspective, ensure that people are working on the most important projects, improve business performance, and provide ample opportunities for development?

The challenge in organizing analytical professionals and semiprofessionals is to get them working "close to the business" on the most important analytical initiatives while keeping them working "close to each other" to coordinate their efforts and for purposes of mutual learning and support.

In our research and discussions with companies, we've found that there may be no single right answer to how to organize your analysts—but there are many wrong ones. So we'll try to help you avoid the common mistakes, while also showing what an organizational model should accomplish.

Companies with a lot of semipros often house them with the functions they serve, so financial analysts work in finance and marketing analysts work in marketing. On the other hand, when semipros are few and multipurpose, they may be grouped with the professionals. Some companies gather them into a centralized unit, so they can work with and learn from each other regularly. Others align their analysts with business units for geographical and administrative convenience. Figure 6-2 depicts five basic options for organizational structure of analytical professionals and

FIGURE 6-2

Options for organizing analytical talent

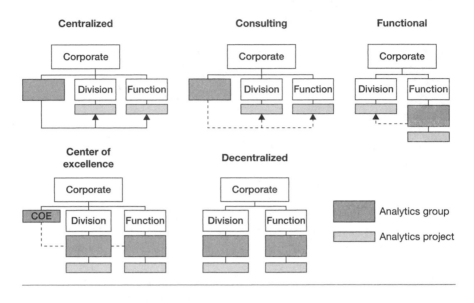

semipros in large, multidivisional corporations. We discuss them in order from the most centralized to the most decentralized.

Centralized. In a centralized model, all analyst groups report to one corporate organization, even if they are assigned to different business units or functions. This centralization makes it easier to deploy analysts on projects with strategic priority; however, it can create distance between analysts and the business, especially if the analysts are all housed in the corporate location. One organization employing this approach is the candy manufacturer Mars, whose centralized Catalyst group has long-term funding and can be deployed strategically to work with any part of the business. Expedia has also recently formed a centralized analyst group.

Consulting. In a consulting model, all analysts are part of one organization, but instead of corporate deploying analysts to business unit projects, the business units "hire" analysts as consultants to their analytical projects. There are several benefits to this model: it is more market driven than the centralized model, and by consolidating its analysts it also enables an enterprisewide view of what's going on. Even more important, it allows the consultants to educate and advise their customers on how to utilize analyst services—in other words, to make the market demand smart. This model falters under weak enterprise focus, poor executive leadership, or faulty targeting mechanisms, all of which create an environment in which analysts end up working on whatever project the business units choose to pay for (or whatever wheel is squeakiest) rather than projects that deliver the most business value. As with the centralized model, analysts may be resident in business units, but they report to the central consulting organization. United Airlines, eBay, and Schneider National all employ the consulting approach.

Functional. In a functional model, a single analyst group resides in whichever department or function is the primary consumer of analyst services, but the group may also provide consulting services to the rest of the corporation. The functional model allows analysts to migrate as analytical applications are completed, and the analytical orientation of the corporation changes. For example, the analytics unit may report first to operations or logistics, then later migrate to marketing. Fidelity, for example, employs the functional approach; the great majority of their analysts work in the "customer knowledge" group, which reports to marketing. However, its analysts can serve other parts of the organization as consultants when needed.

Center of Excellence. In a center of excellence (COE) model, analyst groups are decentralized. They reside in every major business unit or function that has an appetite for analytics, but all groups are members of (and perhaps report dotted line to) a corporate center of excellence for analytics. The COE model builds a community of analysts who can learn from each other by sharing experiences and best practices. Sometimes a strong COE can also double as a "program office," looking across analytical initiatives, advising on project priorities and staffing, and facilitating when analyst groups need to borrow staff from one another. Both Capital One and Bank of America employ versions of this model: at Capital One the "heavy-duty" PhD statisticians are in a center of excellence; Bank of America has analysts spread around the bank, so it tries to overcome the model's limitations by holding regular conferences and running an online portal to encourage communication among analysts.

Decentralized. In a decentralized model, analyst groups are associated with business units and functions without any corporate or consolidating structure. The decentralized model is the most prevalent according to our research, which reflects the immaturity of most corporations' analytical capabilities today. This model makes it difficult to set enterprise priorities and to develop and deploy staff effectively through borrowing and rotation. We've found that the purely decentralized model is effective only in the rare case of a large, diversified, multibusiness corporation in which the businesses have little in common. Because it wouldn't be a compliment, we won't name any companies with decentralized organizational models— but there are plenty of them.

We have also seen variations on these models. Procter & Gamble, for example, starts with a centralized model, consolidating over 120 analysts in a central shared services organization. But the analysts, who are each assigned to a brand or business unit, work at locations around the world. Still other P&G analysts work on a consulting basis. We've also seen "combination" models—like decentralized analytics groups plus a corporate consulting cadre that provides specialized services and supplemental staff to business unit projects. Finally, corporations with autonomous business units often use a "federated" approach that installs analyst groups in each business unit, establishes a corporate group to drive enterprise initiatives, and coordinates all the groups with clear "guidelines of federation."

Of course, the companies we studied all felt that they had sound reasons for the models they chose. The decentralized model emerged as the most popular approach, with 42 percent of respondents.[15] Unlike in high school, however, popularity isn't everything. The ideal model ensures that your scarce and valuable analysts (1) are tasked with the most important analytical projects, (2) bring an enterprise perspective to bear, and (3) have ample opportunities for development and job satisfaction.

We think the centralized and center of excellence models (or a federated model combining elements of both) offer the greatest potential benefit for organizations ready to take an enterprise approach to analytics. Analysts in a centralized or center of excellence model have significantly higher levels of engagement, job satisfaction, perceived organizational support and resources, and intention to stay than decentralized analysts or those who work in consulting units. Centralized and center of excellence organizational models are most common in more sophisticated analytical enterprises. And both models were most often found in the industries that we'd expect to have advanced analytical capabilities, including retail, consumer goods and services, financial services, and health and life sciences.

Company size was less of a factor than type of industry, although we found that companies with fewer than a thousand employees were more likely to organize their analysts into one functional area, while larger companies (with over twenty-five thousand employees) were more likely to operate with a center of excellence model.

Managing Analysts

Vital to the long-term success of any analytically minded organization, analysts are often among the most difficult talent to locate, attract, and retain. However, few companies manage their analytical talent as a strategic resource. Because analysts are often scattered throughout the organization, many companies don't even have a clear picture of who their analysts are, where they reside organizationally or how many they have. They certainly don't recognize or manage them as a distinct and pivotal workforce segment that requires its own recruiting strategies, training and development plans, career paths or performance manage-ment processes. To effectively manage analysts, companies must: (1) de-fine the organization's needs for analytical skills; (2) tap into new and diverse analytical talent pools; (3) develop analytical and business skills; and (4) deploy analysts so that their efforts are aligned with the organi-zation's strategic goals.[16] The following sections describe these four activities.

Defining Resource Needs for Analysts

The first step in defining a company's needs for analysts is to identify analytical capabilities that a company needs to achieve strategic and op-erational goals, determine which analyst jobs are "mission critical," and inventory the analytical talent already in place to fill these needs. Armed with an understanding of their analytical resource requirements and current employee skills, companies can make better use of the analyti-cal talent they have and plan their human resource needs more effec-tively. For example, one global consumer products company predicts its talent needs three years out, based on an understanding of where the business is going and what skills and capabilities will be needed. Bank of America reviewed its employees and identified a subset of its job

FIGURE 6-3

Analytical skill assessment at a retailer

	# analytical resources	Amateurs ▸ Workbench ▸ Standard reports ▸ Alerts	Semiprofessionals ▸ Multidimensional analysis ▸ Analytical applications ▸ Data visualization	Professionals ▸ What-if planning ▸ Predictive modeling ▸ Statistical analysis
Stores	50	Intermediate	Intermediate	Foundational
Buyers	125	Intermediate	Intermediate	Foundational
Supply chain	55	Foundational	Foundational	Foundational
Marketing	74	Foundational	Intermediate	Intermediate
Finance	48	Intermediate	Intermediate	Foundational
Services	25	Foundational	Basic	Basic
HR	12	Foundational	Basic	Basic
Total	389			

Basic · Foundational · Intermediate · Advanced · Expert

descriptions as "analytical." The company ultimately identified over two thousand people as analytical professionals, semipros, or amateurs.

Before hiring for a retailer's many open analytical positions, managers first evaluated the skills already available across the business (see figure 6-3) and compared them to where they were most needed. This review of skills and open positions found many people who were either under- or overqualified for their work. Realigning people with positions reduced the number of new hires and had the added benefit of greatly improving employee job satisfaction and engagement.

Tapping into New Sources of Analysts

Given the growing demand for analysts, astute business leaders must ensure that they can hire or source the necessary skills. Organizations used to recruit analysts just like they sought any other white-collar worker. Now, they must discover novel ways to access analytical skills—from using untapped skills of existing employees to finding new talent pools. Doing so ensures that analytical companies are not locked into particular locations or stuck in shrinking talent pools.

Just as adventurers on safari seek out game at the watering hole, you can most easily find analytical people where they naturally gather—analytics conferences like INFORMS (the operations research society), vendor-sponsored meetings, university groups, and industry interest groups. Analysts often prefer to live near quantitatively oriented universities and major financial centers where their skills are in highest demand. Companies looking for advanced skills may also turn to resources like social networking groups (such as LinkedIn), specialty search firms, and quant Web sites.[7] Even poaching analysts from high-performing competitors has become commonplace.

Getting the best analysts can require flexibility. One manager was able to fill several positions at once by allowing new hires to remain in the small town where they lived after their former employer moved their positions to a large city. Another way to gain access to top analysts is to tailor job descriptions to fit the individual. Kyle Cheek was originally hired into HCSC in the special investigations department, in a position created solely to facilitate the hiring of political economics PhDs. Although he had the analytical skills the company needed, his atypical background could otherwise have prevented his getting a job because he did not fit any position requirements.

Any company seeking an ongoing supply of internal analytics capabilities must also forge tight links with the best graduate school programs worldwide—programs with robust reputations for rigorous training in analytics. Sponsorships and internships can form close relationships with academic institutions. Dow Chemical, for example, enjoys a long-standing partnership with Central Michigan University and hires many of its graduates. Similarly, SAS endowed a Masters in Advanced Analytics program at North Carolina State, and companies have flocked to hire its alumni.

Some organizations go even further to connect with future recruits well before they hit the universities. Texas Instruments joined forces with the National Council of Teachers of Mathematics and CBS to sponsor an education program based on the television program *Numb3rs,* whose story lines are inspired by actual FBI cases in which mathematicians solve crimes and prevent terrorist attacks. By generating interest in math, science, and technology, these analytical organizations promote the development of analytical skills at an early age.

Traditionally, companies have either supplemented in-house analysts with independent contractors or outsourced work to specialist firms in North America or western Europe. But given the talent shortage in these markets, businesses are increasingly looking to emerging markets—such as China and India—to bridge the talent gap. Often underrated as a vast pool of highly educated, cheap number crunchers, these emerging markets are becoming an excellent source of talent as they gain the capabilities and experience to carry out some of the most complex analytical tasks. Leading this trend, India is the fastest-growing market for offshore analytics delivery. By 2011, we estimate that the majority of the offshore market for analytics delivery will be based in India.[18]

Some resourceful organizations have uncovered creative new sources of analysts, proving that your analytics expert does not have to be on your payroll—or even in your home country. For example, some companies are using Web-based "idea marketplaces" such as www.Innocentive.com and www.NineSigma.com to post requests (and rewards) for solutions to their trickiest analytical problems. And Netflix had a competition that offered a top prize of $1 million to whoever can improve by at least 10 percent the accuracy of Cinematch, its movie recommendation algorithm.[19] Even MIT has taken to leaving advanced mathematical equations on its chalkboards after hours, in hopes that one of their janitors happens to be an underachieving quantitative genius. Oh, wait—that may have just been a movie.[20]

Developing Analysts

Analytical techniques and tools are constantly changing, and the skills demanded of analysts at all levels are perpetually being redefined. To respond to this constant flux—not to mention keep analysts engaged—analytical organizations must invest in updating their analysts' skills, particularly those that accelerate strategic business benefits.

One approach is to train analysts internally. Analytical amateurs especially benefit from improving their skills in analytical opportunities, methods, and tools. At Procter & Gamble, for example, the central product supply analytics group offers a course called Analytics with Spreadsheets—often the preferred tool of analytical amateurs. The trucking firm Schneider National's central analytics group offers the courses Introduction to Data Analysis and Statistical Process Control in Services.

Another avenue to increase analytical skills is by rotating developmental assignments. Analysts who routinely analyze the same data and look at the same business problems tend to fall into a rut. Rotational assignments keep them on their toes and help them bring a fresh perspective to different parts of the business. Analytical amateurs also learn well when they have the opportunity to work alongside different pros and semipros on analytics projects. These assignments can be part of a formal job rotation program; when managed well, they can turn their departments into hotbeds of valuable analytical activity. For example, GE Money's offshore analytics centers in Shanghai and Bangalore loan their staff for temporary assignments in business operations through a formal job rotation program. This has aided retention (in very competitive markets) and improved employee engagement by offering analysts new learning opportunities, task variety, and a sense that they are making meaningful contributions to the business. The local businesses see the benefits, too, and demand for these analysts is growing.[21]

Deploying Analysts

Matching a person's skills and aspirations with the jobs the business needs is critical; however, it's no simple trick to find people who can not only deliver the goods today but also develop the skills to deliver different goods tomorrow. Most analytical amateur work and some semipro work is predictable and routine, so if people demonstrate the skills and the company has established performance measures, then matching talent to work is relatively easy. Analytical pros, like PhD statisticians, for example, are another story. Highly educated pros, with rare combinations of knowledge and experience, are in scarce supply. So put your best analysts where they'll do the most good. Make sure that the pros are focused on the company's biggest problems and be prepared to move them around as needed.

Deploying analysts appropriately is a win/win. Analytical people have skills that are in high demand, so organizations should recognize analysts as a special segment of high-value workers whose preferences and motivators are distinct from those of the average employee. Organizations must also connect analysts with one another, especially when they are few or dispersed; creating communities reduces ineffective "pockets of analytics" and facilitates learning.

Managing Analysts Through the Stages

Analytical people may be the last element of the DELTA model, but they are by no means the least important one. An investment in understanding what makes analytical people tick and how to take full advantage of their skills and capabilities has a huge payoff. In the early stages of business analytics, just attending to the care and feeding of your analysts is enough. But as demand builds, the organizational challenges increase.

At each stage, consider how to acquire, develop, engage, organize, develop, and deploy analysts. Recommendations by stage are summarized in table 6-1.

From Stage 1 to Stage 2. Start to identify and assess your existing analysts: who they are, where they reside within the organization, and how deep their analytical skills range. It probably won't take you long! Offer training opportunities aimed at developing analytical expertise—in statistical methods, software tools, and applications. Encourage communication and informal links between analysts and the rest of the organization. Enlist senior business leaders to get to know, appreciate, and engage analytical workers.

From Stage 2 to Stage 3. This transition should mark a more sustained effort to obtain, manage, and develop the best analytical talent. Seek out and nurture specialized recruitment sources (Web sites, associations,

TABLE 6-1

Moving to the next stage: Analysts

From stage 1 Analytically Impaired to stage 2 Localized Analytics	From stage 2 Localized Analytics to stage 3 Analytical Aspirations	From stage 3 Analytical Aspirations to stage 4 Analytical Companies	From stage 4 Analytical Companies to stage 5 Analytical Competitors
Identify pockets of analysts and skills. Offer analytical skills training. Encourage analytical components of systems projects. Enlist managers to appreciate and engage analytical employees.	Define analytical positions and use specialty recruiting sources to fill them. Encourage knowledge sharing among analysts of all types. Promote rotational deployment of analysts. Provide coaching and support, especially for analytical professionals.	Evaluate analytical expertise of all information workers, develop relationships with universities and associations, and provide advanced training for analysts. Focus on developing business acumen in analysts and analytical expertise in business executives. Integrate the development and deployment process. Form communities of analysts.	Hire analytically minded employees in all business roles. Formalize an analyst-role/business-role rotation program. Organize and deploy analysts centrally. Regularly recognize analytical employees in all roles, and ensure that analysts are constantly challenged in their work.

academic contacts) that target analysts. Customize job descriptions to attract analytical skills and know-how. Encourage networking among analysts of all levels—champions, professionals, semiprofessionals, and amateurs—to share knowledge and skills. Move people who work on similar topics closer together to encourage collaboration and drive efficiency. Support and coach analysts in data-heavy roles—this will help you see how to improve training and development. Finally, foster general business and industry expertise in analytical talent.

From Stage 3 to Stage 4. Build links with academia and industry associations in order to gain access to future recruits and specialized skills. Provide training and development opportunities for professionals and semiprofessionals to keep them up-to-date with the newest processes, software, and technologies. Champion the use of analytics within your organization by developing business acumen in your analytical professionals and analytical knowledge in your business executives. Create wider communities for your analysts, spanning corporate functions, business units, and geographies. These communities allow analysts to keep up-to-date with the latest developments in analytics, solve common problems, and discover opportunities. If feasible, centralize your key analysts.

From Stage 4 to Stage 5. Tailor your HR strategy and processes around analytically minded employees—even incoming amateurs should display a basic level of analytical expertise. Provide interesting and challenging work to attract, engage, and retain outstanding analytical talent. Implement a rotation program to give them greater exposure to the challenges facing different functions, business units, and geographies. Adapt performance management processes to reflect your expectations of analysts, thereby ensuring that your analytical talent will receive recognition for their work.

Keep in Mind . . .

- Top quants are scarce resources, not human calculators. Analysts can feel isolated from their business colleagues and overlooked when it comes to their contributions. They are likely to depart for greener pastures when they feel unappreciated.

- Analytical workers are motivated by interesting and challenging work, not by large paychecks alone.

- Offshore resources, professors and their graduate students, and open competitions are innovative sources of analytic talent. Seek a variety of talented analysts by cultivating sources like universities, social networking sites, and conferences.

- Hire employees with analytical aptitude and give them the training they need to use analytics well.

- Organize and deploy your analysts strategically to leverage their skills across the enterprise, whether in a centralized group or on rotation across the organization.

- Analytics is a broad field of knowledge: analytical amateurs, semipros, and professionals require quantitative and technical skills, industry expertise, and business acumen; but they also need the skills to communicate effectively, build relationships, and coach others.

Part Two

STAYING ANALYTICAL

To unleash the full power of business analytics and sustain it over time, you have to make it part of how people across the organization work, manage, and think every day. Many stage 4 or 5 companies we've worked with have the DELTA elements in place, and analytical applications are boosting performance and competitiveness, but only in one or two areas of the business, often marketing and logistics. Meanwhile, the organization at large does not employ analytics, and may be puzzled by what they are and why they matter.

We're not suggesting that everyone in the company must be analytical, simply that the more analytical amateurs a company has, the merrier. And we're not suggesting that all business activities need formal models—after all, the purpose of having an enterprise view and targets is to focus attention and efforts where the payback is greatest. We are saying that a company's operations, decision making, and performance can be improved in countless small ways if more employees know how to find relevant data, analyze it, make sounder decisions, and manage by fact. Analytical thinking should be less the exception and more the rule across the business.

Companies that are truly becoming analytical have three hallmarks:

1. *Analytics are **embedded** in major business processes, the "workhorse" activities of the enterprise.* Early decision support systems were intended to help managers report, analyze, and interpret data to make better decisions. But such applications rarely had a significant impact because the tools weren't integrated with business

applications and work processes. Managers who wanted to use them had to interrupt their work to perform an analysis. Embedding is a better approach: design automated processes around repetitive decisions (like auto insurance pricing) that have well-defined criteria. Chapter 7 discusses what kinds of business processes lend themselves to embedding analytics and presents specific techniques for doing so.

2. *The company builds and continually reinforces a **culture** of analytical decisions, a "test and learn" philosophy, and a commitment to fact-based decision making.* Managers in analytical cultures are not satisfied with guesses about what works. Merit triumphs over politics, so managers are encouraged to push back when someone proposes a project that lacks data to back it up. In an analytical culture, asking tough questions is the norm, and leadership from the top is critical. As one analytically oriented executive told us, "It is not my job to have all the answers, but it is my job to ask lots of penetrating, disturbing, and occasionally almost offensive questions as part of the analytic process that leads to insight and refinement."[1] When that kind of attitude spreads through an organization, analytical cultures thrive. Chapter 8 details the characteristics of an analytical culture and how to nourish one.

3. *Never satisfied, and always mindful of how business conditions change, the company continually **reviews** its business assumptions and analytical models.* An analytical capability should be no more static than the business world in which it operates. Failure to adapt can be disastrous: consider how U.S. airlines, once pioneers in the use of analytical models for yield management and logistics, lost their competitive edge; or how subprime mortgage providers developed analytical models that worked well when housing prices were rising, only to see the roof cave in when prices fell precipitously. Strategically, you need to review and renew the fit among objectives, business models, and analytical approaches. Tactically, you need to review analytical models. Data sources, emerging technologies, market assumptions and model parameters all need to be reviewed periodically to keep models fresh. Chapter 9 details how to "close the loop" by being clear-eyed and vigilant about managing your use of analytics.

These three characteristics are especially important once you reach stage 3 of your analytical journey. You simply won't be able to take analytics to the next stage or to sustain analytical momentum across leadership changes unless a critical mass of employees are thinking and working analytically. In sum, these three characteristics distinguish organizations that merely undertake a series of individual analytical projects from those that build a long-term analytical capability, that truly become analytical.

7

EMBED ANALYTICS IN BUSINESS

PROCESSES

IF YOU REALLY WANT to put analytics to work in an enterprise, you need to make them an integral part of everyday business decisions and business processes—the methods by which work gets done and value gets created. In an analytical enterprise, analytics can't be relegated to a few quants squirreled away in the basement. Nor should a few isolated applications be reserved for special occasions like marketing campaigns. Rather, analytical applications and tools must be used routinely by information workers as a natural part of their daily work. When embedded in processes and workflow, analytics shift from being an occasional ancillary activity to being a consistent, routine, and natural part of doing business. Embedding analytics into processes improves the ability of the organization to implement new insights. It eliminates gaps between insights, decisions, and actions.

The car rental company Avis Europe narrowed the gap considerably when it embedded analytics into its reservation process, for instance. Profitability in the car rental business depends on distributing an exact number of cars to the right places for the customers who will pay the best price. Traditionally, the company would rely upon the experience and judgment of its fleet managers, asking them to study the data in the reservation system each week to predict which areas would have the greatest demand for cars. Yet according to Avis director of station systems Jens Utech, the company fell into a rut, using the same routines year after year. For example, every Friday morning one station manager would transport a truckload of cars from Heathrow Airport to downtown London in anticipation of the weekend rush—with no idea of how many cars would actually be needed. According to Utech, there was no way to see how the company could improve; too many decisions about distribution and pricing were made with "no forecast and no sophistication."

In an attempt to make better and more transparent decisions about fleet distribution, the company tested out an analytical program in the reservation process. Within a year, the program was able to use data from Avis's reservation system to forecast precisely where cars would be needed. For example, rather than send a truckload of cars from Heathrow to London on Friday morning, the program might forecast that the fleet would be best utilized by sending four cars from Heathrow Airport and another four from nearby Stansted Airport. Aside from this more exact fleet management, the system also suggested ways to optimize reservations. During busy seasons like Christmas, for example, reservations may be restricted to customers renting for a minimum of three days; that way, cars would be more likely to be available for the most profitable customers. Similarly, the system helps managers to predict when a certain station might run out of cars, so they can raise prices in advance. By embedding analytics directly into everyday decision making, the company increased its fleet utilization by two points, or $19 million.[1]

As compelling as the economic benefits are, the underlying power of analytics comes in *making connections*—recognizing patterns in business activities, isolating the drivers of performance, and anticipating the effects of decisions and actions. To make connections, you must look beyond the immediate task or decision and appreciate what happens "upstream" and "downstream." That is, you must examine how analytics fit into the entire business process.

Applying analytics to a particular function helps to determine things like the optimal advertising spending for a product. But even more compelling to a marketing executive is when the spending can be optimized across multiple advertising channels, different geographies, and the company's full range of products. To accomplish this broader perspective, we must focus analytics on the entire marketing process, not just a piece of it.

And looking at a single process is really just the beginning. We've noted before that to really maximize business performance you need an enterprise perspective. A cross-functional process perspective enables you to appreciate how different parts of the business work together (or fail miserably in doing so) and to identify all the ways analytics might be used to create a better outcome for the enterprise. From this perspective you can see how people, processes, and technologies work together to promote the best possible decisions and to execute those decisions efficiently. Manufacturers, for example, may invest in product life-cycle management software to coordinate information and analytically based decisions across a product's life cycle from R&D through retirement, affecting nearly every process in the business.

Craft Versus Industrial Analytics

The earliest application of analytics in any business is invariably for a special occasion when the need for more information and analysis is palpable. Even today, a lot of analytical effort employs the "craft" approach, where each decision is its own ad hoc effort. There's nothing wrong with this approach—it's appropriate for any new analytical decision. However, as decisions (even complex ones) become familiar, well understood, and routine, you may subject them to an "industrial-strength" approach. The industrial approach automates and integrates analytics into decision-based work processes—and all without any of the labor violations and environmental pollution inherent to most industrialization processes.

Table 7-1 contrasts the craft and industrial approaches to employing business analytics. Craft is a one-time effort, inherently limited in effect. Industrial takes more time and effort up front, but later the decisions can be instantaneous. With craft, the analysis is often discarded or forgotten after use. With the industrial approach, analytical models and rules are a seamless part of the process used to execute decisions.

Three Types of Decisions

To take an industrial approach, you must decide how extensively analytically enabled decisions should be automated. There are three fundamental approaches.[2] With the *fully automated approach,* the system makes the decision and sets in motion subsequent process flow. If the decision is well defined, decision rules are clear, and the policy is "no exceptions," then the decision can be automated. If instantaneous response time is needed, then the decision *must* be automated. Yield

TABLE 7-1

"Craft" versus "industrial" analytics

	Craft	Industrial
Pattern	Ad hoc, project-oriented	Embedded in an ongoing process
Purpose	One-time decision or event support	Ongoing process performance
Benefit	One-time	Recurring
Investment	Lower, one-time	Higher up front, recurring to maintain the decision model
Time to implement	Relatively brief	Longer
Speed of analysis	Same as time to implement	Once implemented, fast or instantaneous
Staff	Labor-intensive	Labor-intensive up front, modest ongoing effort to maintain
Memory of analysis	Can be saved for reuse, but is often lost	Maintained and improved upon

management systems in hotels and airlines and loan and insurance underwriting systems in financial services are good examples of analytical decisions that are often fully automated.

Second is the *exceptions/overrides approach.* When a decision covers a wide variety of cases, most of which are standard but some of which are exceptions that demand expertise and judgment, the standard decisions can be automated, but a person should be alerted to examine the exceptions. The trick here is setting the parameters that define exceptions, and determining whether the person needs to quickly review the standard decisions as well as the exceptions. Insurance companies, for example, often invoke human experts when an insurance policy application is particularly large or complex. Too bad this approach wasn't used in the *Terminator* and *Matrix* movies: with it, computer systems could have been overridden before they were able to enslave humanity!

Third is the *assisted approach.* If the decision is very complex (e.g., how to structure a financial deal), involves unpredictable variables (e.g., customer reactions), is unprecedented (e.g., new business models), or requires the expertise of a variety of people and disciplines, then the role of analytics is to assist and inform the decision, not to make it. In medical processes, for example, the physician may first consider an automated recommendation but then make up his or her own mind about how to treat a patient. Ideally, such systems provide a rich set of relevant information and analysis and perhaps a simulation of process flow and results for the decision makers to use. And these more ad hoc, independent models are maintained, improved, and made available for reuse.

Table 7-2 summarizes and contrasts these different methods of enabling decisions. Any given business process may incorporate all three decision types. It will take iterative design, testing, and implementation to determine the best mix in decision design. And note that decisions may migrate toward automated over time as key variables are isolated and understood and as patterns of exceptions are recognized and modeled.

Determining the right mix of fully automated decisions, automated decisions with human review, and human decisions informed by analytics takes careful consideration. Your company should ask the following questions: Should a decision be fully automated, or should a person have the power to override a recommended decision? Should the system generate alerts or automatic updates (e.g., informing customers about the status of actions on their behalf)? Should humans who override the analytical recommendation be penalized, or interviewed to find out their reasoning? The answers to these questions will put you well on the path toward embedding analytics into processes, and ultimately achieving analytical process nirvana.

TABLE 7-2

Three types of decisions

	Automated	Automated with overrides	Assisted
Decision types	Simple and/or well-defined	Bell-curve distribution of decision complexity	Complex
Exception handling	No exceptions	Exceptions are recognizable and get special handling	Unpredictable variables must be accommodated
Key ingredients	Speed and consistency	Expertise	Expertise and collaboration
Analytics focus	Rules	Alerts	Simulation

Analytical Process Nirvana

How does a truly analytically enabled business process work? We describe its ideal characteristics as "analytical process nirvana":

- We know the key decision points in the process.

- We have the information to enable each decision that may come from upstream or downstream in the process, from elsewhere in the business, or from the marketplace.

- We rely on analytical techniques and base decisions on facts.

- We employ analytical technologies such as spreadsheets, forecasts, or predictive models to inform, enable, or automatically make each decision.

- Analytical activities and technologies are integrated into the operational systems and processes.

- The process structure and flow are flexible. There are likely different paths, or "lanes," through the process—for example, a fully automated "express lane" for the simple and standard cases, a "regular lane" for automated decisions that are reviewed by a person, and a "specials lane" for unfamiliar or complex cases that demand an experienced decision maker.

- We monitor the performance of these decision systems—and of the process as a whole—with the help of analytics, and we can quickly recognize and act upon the need or opportunity for further process improvement.

Few business processes today approach this state of nirvana. But it's easy to see how they might. Consider claims processing in the insurance industry. Figure 7-1 depicts the key steps and decision points in a claims process for a property and casualty insurance business. The process incorporates a series of analyses and automated or partially automated decisions. The basic process flow—from notification of a claim to closing it—is represented by the boxes with rounded corners and connecting lines. The automated points at which analytics are applied are represented by rectangles.

These decision points fall in three categories. The initial decisions improve the claims process flow itself; the first one serves the customer

FIGURE 7-1

Embedded analytics in a claims process

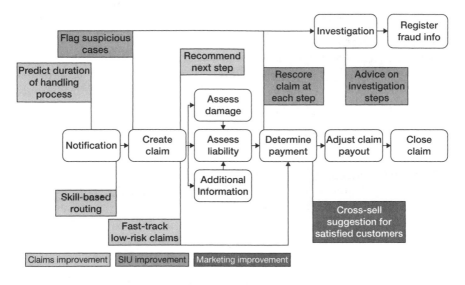

Source: Based on "Predictive Analytics for the Claim Handling Process." SPSS Inc. Technical Report, 2009.

by predicting how long the claim and payment are likely to take. Another uses the preliminary information in the notification to route the claim depending on the level of skill needed to process it. Once the claim is created the process branches into two paths. One decision point routes the simple cases, those with a low risk of fraud, to a "fast track" resolution and payment. The other recommends the degree to which additional damage assessment and other information are needed to assess liability. At various points in the process flow, the claim is "scored" for likelihood of fraud; a high score directs the claim to a special investigations unit (SIU) with suggested investigative actions. Finally, toward the end of the process, a recommendation engine suggests cross-selling opportunities (e.g., for improvements in coverage) at or after the point when a satisfied customer receives payment.

The result is a process that is simultaneously efficient and flexible—the fast track reduces effort, only complex claims receive the full assessment, and only likely fraud is investigated. In fact, the process is efficient *because* it is flexible, with analytically determined variations in the process flow. Even with capital-intensive processes (e.g., a manufacturer's supply chain), companies have learned that the flexible process beats the rigidly optimized one in the long run. A process fine-tuned to operate just one way inevitably paints the business into a corner when market demand or other conditions change. Through instantaneous, informed, consistent, and automated decisions, embedded analytics enable a wide variety of business processes to be much more flexible while operating faster and more efficiently. Of course, as in the claims processing example, it's hard to achieve these process benefits without excellent analytics and information technology.

You will, of course, want to make your own assessment of the analytical potential of your business processes. (And if your memory is short or you're skipping around, look back at chapter 5 for ideas and techniques on targeting applications.) The real-time and institutional action applications on the top two rungs of the applications ladder particularly benefit from being embedded into ongoing processes. Consider where the heightened speed, efficiency, and flexibility afforded by embedding analytics into processes and real-time applications will have the greatest potential for market differentiation.

You might also want to gauge the difference between the current level of analytical support and the analytical potential of each process. You're likely to find opportunities everywhere—the challenge is to ensure that the opportunities, if exploited, will truly drive business performance and competitive advantage. And keep in mind that ad hoc or "craft" analytics will still play an important role in conjunction with processes that may not be ready for embedded or "industrial" analytics.

Embedded Analytics in Action

We see examples of analytics at work within core processes in a variety of business areas. Statistical analysis has been a feature of supply chain and logistics management for decades, starting with the techniques of statistical process control (SPC) and total quality management (TQM). Real-time analytics are helping guide call center workers in their interactions with customers. And analytics are well established in the engineering and simulation sides of product design.

Among business support functions, analytics are essential to many facets of finance, common in the management of technology operations, and relatively new to human resources (though of enormous potential there). In corporate development, key decisions—for example, regarding mergers and acquisitions—may benefit greatly from analytics, but few companies take a process approach to such activities.

Consider the example of UPS to whet your appetite for embedding analytics in your core business processes. As a logistics company, UPS lives and breathes the "traveling salesman problem"—how to reach a variable series of destinations most efficiently with the right delivery capacity, and often in designated time windows, every day. The solutions naturally demand very sophisticated and industrialized analytics: for capacity planning of aircraft and truck fleets, for routing packages through its distribution network, and for scheduling and routing delivery trucks. For a company this steeped in analytical applications, the frontier is moving closer to real-time, dynamic adjustments. For example, UPS is experimenting with algorithms to adjust the order of deliveries as conditions (e.g., road closures, extraordinary customer need) change.

Making Processes Analytical

The effects of analytics on the operations of a process can be profound, and over time you may want to reengineer the overall business process and revamp its information systems to capitalize on the potential for analytics-based improvement. But you can start embedding analytics without a major overhaul. For processes that rely extensively on enterprise systems, it may be possible to simply start taking advantage of the analytical capabilities that are already included in the software. However, many process analytics initiatives will require tools, techniques, and working relationships that are likely to be new and unfamiliar at first. We have found that implementing analytics-enabled processes requires applying four major perspectives.

The first is *process implementation*. Occasionally a business may create a new analytically enabled process or rebuild a process from scratch, but most often you are adding capability to and altering an existing process. Especially given the iterative nature of many analytical applications, it's essential to measure baseline process performance first and to run the enhanced process in parallel to the original (perhaps as a pilot or test) in order to refine the new process and measure its performance and value. In some cases, process simulation can yield insights about how the process might perform even before implementation.

Next, organizations should consider *model implementation*. Much of the distinctive work of process analytics centers on designing, developing, and iteratively refining statistical algorithms and descriptive or predictive models or rule-based systems. If you are going to industrialize important decision processes, it is important that the rules, assumptions, and algorithms in your model are correct. Analytical projects generally require different tools and development methodologies from those employed in more traditional systems development. And, of course, this work is performed by business analysts and programmers with special skills in statistical methods and modeling.

Third is *systems implementation*. The analytical system must be incorporated into the set of systems and technologies supporting the business process. In building these interfaces, it helps to employ process-oriented technologies, including capabilities of ERP systems, workflow, and document management systems. And integrating and testing the new systems and interfaces is critical given analytics' reliance on a broad range of quality data and the fact that analytics-based decisions may dramatically change process flow.

Human implementation is the fourth perspective. Often the greatest implementation challenge, especially when analytics is new to the process and the people performing it, is on the human side. Only people can tell if an embedded application is resulting in good decisions, so be sure to involve them in developing, managing, and monitoring the assumptions and results of any embedded model. Another important factor is developing the right mix of automated and human decision making and enabling process performers to trust and use their new analytical information and sometimes tools.

All four perspectives must mesh: process flow and decisions are enabled or controlled by analytical models, other information systems interface with the models and provide clean data feeds, and people perform the process better with the help of embedded analytics. If you lack clear business goals, specifications, or momentum, be prepared to demo or pilot the concept, to work with stakeholders to define targets and set ambitions, and to make the business case for investing in prerequisite assets, often starting with data.

IT's Role in Embedding Analytics into Business Processes

Technology is an integral part of most business processes today. So the best route to embedding analytics into processes is often through the technologies and applications that employees routinely use to do their jobs. Embedding analytics into processes starts with a robust analytical architecture that provides an accurate, timely, standardized, integrated, secure, and reliable information management environment. Scorecards and applications that monitor and alert based on predetermined thresholds are the norm these days, but too many remain as standalone applications. An industrial-strength IT architecture makes it vastly easier to weave analytics into ongoing work processes in three ways:

1. *Automated decision applications.* These sense online data or conditions, apply codified knowledge or logic, and make decisions—all with minimal human intervention. Technology is best suited to automate decisions that must be made frequently and rapidly, using any kind of information (data, text, images) that is available electronically. The knowledge and decision criteria used in these systems need to be highly structured. The factors that must be taken into account (the business problem's dimensions, conditions, and decision factors) must be clearly understood and not subject to rapid obsolescence. The conditions are ripe for automating the decision when experts can readily codify the decision rules, a production system automates the surrounding process, and high-quality data exists in electronic form. Business activities that benefit from automated decision-making applications include fraud detection, solution configuration, yield optimization, recommendation/real-time offers, dynamic forecasting, and operational control (like monitoring and adjusting temperature).

2. *Business applications for operational and tactical decision making.* Analytical managers rely on analytical applications (whether custom developed or from third parties) that are integrated directly into Web applications or enterprise systems for tasks such as supply chain optimization, sales forecasting, and advertising effectiveness/planning. Recommendation, planning, and "what-if" applications can incorporate near real-time information and multiple models to dynamically optimize a solution while factoring in conflicting goals like profitability and customer satisfaction. Analytical business applications are best suited to well-defined, periodic tasks in which most of the information needed is predictable and available electronically. Since

the data, knowledge, and decision criteria are typically less defined and/or more fluid than those of a fully automated application, they require industry and functional expertise.

3. *Information workflow, project management, collaboration, and personal productivity tools.* Most information work is done through
personal productivity tools like Microsoft Office. As vendors increase the analytical quotient of their collaboration and productivity tools, analytics become more accessible to analytical amateurs
throughout the enterprise. One consumer products company
found that its elaborate modeling tool was ignored by nearly everyone until the findings were distilled into a monthly deck of ten
PowerPoint slides and e-mailed directly to the sales force. As platform vendors align their products to work together more seam-
lessly, a manager needn't know that his Excel spreadsheet is using
the company's ERP system to prepare his forecast. These tools
and applications work best for less structured information with
less defined decision criteria.

To address the growing need to embed analytics into processes, both
specialty applications vendors and the major platform vendors are building more analytical functionality directly into their tools and applications.
Software companies are building more industry-specific, process-driven
applications. Major platform providers like Oracle are embedding analytics into their products by building statistical functions directly into their
enterprise data warehouse products. ERP vendors, which are including
more sophisticated analytical features, remain a powerful way to integrate
industry best practices into business processes. And Microsoft, Oracle,
SAP, and SAS continue to quietly embed more sophisticated analytics
and business intelligence capabilities into their applications and tools.

Overcoming "Sticking Points" to Embedding Analytics

In the course of our research, we talked with a variety of people experienced in embedding analytics into business processes, from first forays
to applications with competitive impact. We'll leave you with a list, com-
piled from the insights of these seasoned practitioners, of seven of
the most common obstacles, or "sticking points," specific to embedded
analytics implementations.

Specifications. Where do you start if the analytics are entirely new to the process and it's difficult to envision how they might work? Or if nobody can really articulate how the decisions currently get made? Undocumented decision methods are very common, often in cases where process performers are very experienced. Key to getting over this sticking point is the skill of your analysts—both working with people to understand their work methods and mental processes, and working with data to tease out its patterns and meaning.

Data. What do you do if important information is incomplete or unavailable, or if stakeholders don't agree on its meaning and format? These are common business and systems problems, the bane of information management professionals everywhere. But they are especially damaging to embedded analytics initiatives because of their reliance on complete and high-quality data. Long-term, the key here is of course to get data assets well organized into a robust representation of the business—and to assess your data management methods on an ongoing basis. Short-term, you may be cleaning up data and trying to analyze it simultaneously. Even the best-structured processes still have missing or "dirty" data on occasion; this is often the reason why semiautomated decisions get "kicked out" to human decision makers.

Business Relationships. How do you articulate plans and progress to process owners and other senior managers and stakeholders who may not be experienced with business analytics or the experimental nature of analytical implementations? This kind of explanation can often feel like a high-stakes game of charades. In particular, algorithm and model development may be a "black box" to key players (leading to a reluctance to make decisions based on the results), or they may expect to see progress and progress reports similar to those of more traditional projects. In these circumstances, several companies report success through careful communication and education efforts. Assess each player's understanding of business analytics and analytical initiatives, and let them know what to expect at each stage of the implementation game.

User Training. How do you wean people off decisions that they've long been making, enable them to trust the analytics, and make them comfortable with the fact that the automated decisions may be more consistent and better informed than theirs? The key here is to incorporate the process performers as early as is realistic in designing and testing the new systems and process, given that they may be untrained and unsophisticated analytically. Then make sure you have feedback channels so process performers can be heard during and after implementation.

Rollout. If the business is decentralized, how do you roll out the new analytically enhanced systems, decision methods, and process to organizations with widely varying analytical capability—and attitudes toward analytics? Do you start where the environment is friendliest, the responsible manager most enthusiastic and committed? Where the revised process will get its most realistic exercising? Where the feedback from process performers and their management is going to be most useful? You seldom find a location that meets all these criteria. Keeping in mind that the first implementation is also going to be an iteration of analytics and process design, we recommend placing more emphasis than usual on getting high-quality feedback.

Completeness. How do you know when you're done? When it's time to declare the implementation complete and shift from iterative construction to model management? Unfortunately, you can't stick a fork in an analytics implementation, or throw one at the wall to see if it hangs there. If the analysts building the application or the business people sponsoring it are perfectionists, then they may be tempted to tweak the application indefinitely. And the business process may continue to improve as a result, but have you reached the point of diminishing returns, and should your analysts be more productively engaged working on other processes and projects? There are two ways to mark completeness. One is to set a process performance target, and when that is reached (or progress toward it slows), declare the implementation over. The other is to have renewable funding for each iteration of design and implementation. When the business sponsor does not anticipate enough added value to fund another round of development, then the project is done.

Transparency. How much of the analytical methods and application do you want to reveal or share, especially when the process involves customers or other business partners? This is a subtle and important point, especially when the analytical application is delivering high business value, perhaps competitive advantage. The tendency has long been to treat such processes and information systems as highly proprietary.

However, the trend in business relationships is strongly toward collaboration, including the integration of processes and systems with those of customers and suppliers. Ask yourself periodically whether you can unleash more business value by sharing your analytical capability than by holding it close—particularly if your own organization's analytical culture would be difficult to emulate easily. The details of your algorithms and models may remain trade secrets, but the process capabilities they enable may best be shared.

Organizations that effectively manage these sticking points, while embedding analytics into core processes and systems, begin to approach "process nirvana." These organizations thoroughly understand workflow, information flow, and decision points for targeted business processes, especially those that are part of their distinctive capability. They leverage analytics to improve efficiency and flexibility simultaneously, and to deliver high performance in the eyes of the process's customers. Embedding analytics into business processes sends a clear signal to employees that analytics are important to the entire organization. The next step to institutionalizing an analytical capability is to embed analytics into the organization's culture. Of course, just as we don't often achieve nirvana in our personal lives, few organizations attain embedded analytical nirvana. But we must all strive for spiritual and analytical perfection.

8

BUILD AN ANALYTICAL CULTURE

WHENEVER WE GO TO A COMPANY that is really good at analytics, we find that an analytical orientation is deeply embedded into its culture. The principles of an analytical culture go beyond the particular attitudes of individual decision makers, and they're rarely communicated as lists of precepts; they're usually things that people just know. In organizations with an analytical culture, new hires, who are selected in part for their analytical skills, quickly find out that the organization runs on analytical and fact-based decisions. While most firms haven't consciously cultivated analytical cultures in the past, we believe that they will increasingly do so in the future.

Analytical Traits and Behaviors

Culture, of course, is one of the softer elements of an organization's makeup, one that may seem incompatible with the "hard" nature of analytics. But it's incredibly critical if you want your firm to make better decisions. What is an analytical culture? Like any culture, it's the sum total of a series of individual attributes and behaviors that get repeated over time. People in an analytical culture demonstrate a set of common attributes. In our research and experience, they

Search for the Truth. Analytically minded people don't accept traditional actions as "given," but try to find out what's really true about how a business operates. They use analytics and data not to appear rational and objective, but to actually *be* rational and objective about the business environment. In their quest for truth, they are intent on applying rigorous objective logic, without preconditions or bias. This means that analysts must question the status quo, common assumptions, and conventional wisdom. As a result, they may arrive at unexpected conclusions, some of which may be politically incorrect. Thus, an analytical culture is a meritocracy that recognizes and rewards the best data-driven insights. People are open to being surprised and thus inclined toward innovation.

Find or Identify Patterns and Get to Root Causes. Work at identifying patterns in data or real-world situations, regardless of your level of ability. Identifying root causes for problems is not just an individual task, but one that can be built into a corporate culture. Toyota's "Five Whys" approach to finding root causes, for example, is deeply embedded. As one executive points out, in Toyota's analytical culture the answers must come not only through deduction, but also through diligent pursuit of each "why?"[1]

Are as Granular as Possible in Their Analysis. Better analytics usually result from more detailed data and analysis. If there is an average in your business, try to "de-average" and understand its variations. If you're using zip code data, try to get census tract or even household data. If you're working with households, try to learn more about the individuals who make up the household.

Seek Data, Not Just Stories, to Analyze a Question or Issue. Non-analytical cultures use stories and anecdotes to support their decisions; analytical cultures seek data. They know that anecdotal evidence may be interesting, but it often isn't representative. That said, allow us to support this point with an anecdote: Memorial Hermann, the largest hospital system in Texas, has become increasingly analytical over time. However, an executive at one of its eleven hospitals commented at a leadership meeting that a major influencer of patient satisfaction and perception of quality was the taste of food. The analytics group at Memorial Hermann examined their own patient satisfaction data to discover whether this was true. In fact, the quality of food was one of the poorest predictors of patient satisfaction. Using regression and examining correlation coefficients, it was actually dead last in a list of over thirty correlates of patient satisfaction. It turns out that the executive had spoken with two patients at his hospital who were grumpy about their food. Rooting out plausible but unsubstantiated explanations of poor performance is vital to make and sustain improvement in health care. That's a major reason why Memorial Hermann won the 2009 National Quality Forum award for achieving exceptional patient outcomes.[2]

Value Negative Results as Well as Positive. Since an analytical orientation is the application of the scientific method to business, one key principle of the scientific method applies: negative results are just as useful as positive ones. That is, if you find out that an intervention doesn't work—it doesn't lift sales or get a customer to buy something from you—that's just as useful as knowing that something does work. A culture that is not receptive to negative results will lead people to skew results in a positive direction—a highly unfortunate cultural attribute!

Use the Results of Analyses to Make Decisions and Take Actions. Making decisions based on power and politics rather than on objective analysis is a cancer on the organizational culture. It suggests that if you are powerful enough in the hierarchy, you'll get your way. This has been one of the problems at General Motors over the years (according to interviews with executives there)—market studies were done, data was gathered, and recommendations were made to management, but they were often ignored in favor of power and politics. Contrast this culture with Procter & Gamble's, where analysts are evaluated not by the quality of their analyses and the answers they develop, but by the breakthrough results that are achieved by putting their ideas into action.

Are Pragmatic About Trade-offs in Decision Making. One of the most common questions we get about analytical decision making is, "Isn't it possible to be too analytical—to gather too much data, or take too long to decide?" Of course it is possible, and it happens frequently. Gathering large amounts of data or doing detailed analysis can sometimes be an excuse for postponing decision and action. The best practitioners in analytical cultures are pragmatic about this trade-off, gathering data and employing analytics when possible, but not delaying unnecessarily to wait for them. If the decision needs to be made quickly, they make it quickly based on experience and the best data available.

An analytical culture comprises many attributes that may be particularly difficult to achieve. Furthermore, the culture may vary by degrees within an organization's departments, functions, business units, and geographies. If you're trying to make your organization more analytical, you need to assess where that culture is prevalent, and where it isn't.

Pushbacks and Pats on the Back

It's still unusual for large numbers of people in large organizations to display the proclivities we've just described. Therefore, organizations that want to establish an analytical culture have to incorporate some firm (but not punitive) "pushbacks" for people who adopt the wrong behaviors. These day-to-day reminders that data and analysis are necessary to make good decisions help people internalize an analytical culture.

At Google, for example, if you bring an idea for a new feature or capability to product management, the first question will be, "Did you do a test or use data?" With its search engine and other applications, Google has what some would consider a terrifying amount of data available from millions of user interactions, so there is no excuse for not using it to make decisions. The same pushbacks will be found at Capital One, eBay, and other highly analytical firms where testing and the use of information are key components of the culture.

Over time, this question needs to be asked less and less, because it becomes baked into the culture. If managers continually come back with the question, colleagues should begin to ask it as well. Eventually only new employees—or existing ones with a memory lapse—would propose an idea without data to support it. Although it's important to occasionally allow an employee to say, "I don't have data to support this, but I think we should consider it anyway," firms with an analytical bent will try to think of a way to test or gather data to support almost any plausible idea.

The "obligation to dissent" is a cousin of the pushback. Some companies (Intel is a prominent example) encourage employees to dissent when they have opinions—or even better, data—supporting an alternative view to the one being proposed. Of course, dissenting has its limits: at Intel the dissent is supposed to end when the decision is made and the participants leave the room.

Senior managers, of course, are most responsible for creating cultures of informed dissent. Michael Roberto, a professor who studies effective decision processes, describes the problem well:

> Consider the nature and quality of dialogue within many organizations. Candor, conflict, and debate appear conspicuously absent during their decision-making processes. Managers feel uncomfortable expressing dissent, groups converge quickly on a particular solution, and individuals assume that unanimity exists when, in fact, it does not. As a result, critical assumptions remain untested, and creative alternatives do not surface or receive adequate attention. In all too many cases, the problem begins with the person directing the process, as their words and deeds discourage a vigorous exchange of views. Powerful, popular, and highly successful leaders hear "yes" much too often, or they simply hear nothing when people really mean "no."[3]

Culture is established not only by pushing back against the wrong behaviors, but also by celebrating the right ones. For an analytical culture, a person who solves a particularly important problem with analytics deserves praise, reminding others that analytics are a path to fame and fortune. Pats on the back are no less valuable than pushbacks.

Analytics in Support of Other Cultures

Ideally, analytics should be combined with other cultural priorities. If your organization is fanatical about developing new products (as is Procter & Gamble), a complementary analytical culture can encourage the development of new product metrics to assess customer reactions and measure how new products are faring in the marketplace —analytical approaches that P&G employs. Companies may also use analytics to support a strong engineering culture, as at Air Products and Chemicals; a strong focus on disciplined financial performance, as at Marriott; or a strong focus on customers, as at Hotels.com, a business unit of Expedia, Inc.

Hotels.com allows customers not only to browse and book hotel rooms, but also to read reviews from previous guests; the site has over a million guest reviews. The company's management decided in 2006 to change its strategy and culture. The site was known as a low-cost way to book hotels, but when the market changed, executives wanted to shift its emphasis to customer service and loyal customer relationships. The company eliminated change and cancellation fees, developed a loyalty program with a free night's stay for each ten nights booked, redesigned its Web site, improved its Web search capabilities, and hired Joe Megibow as vice president of customer experience and online marketing.

Hotels.com is fanatical about gathering and analyzing Web usage statistics, and analysis of that data drives almost everything on its site—a pretty common approach for online firms. But Megibow and other executives felt that basic Web activity and financial reports—all of which showed solid growth and increased sales—were not getting at the truth of the customer experience. Further investigation revealed that the strong numbers were masking a range of problems on the site. By instituting a serious "voice of the customer" program combined with Web analytics, Megibow began to reveal the true story of how customers experienced the site.

The program allowed customers to indicate problems at any time in a session, using software that records every screen presented to a user and which mouse clicks a customer makes (don't worry, philanderers: this information isn't for sale). The company even created separate phone numbers (more than seven hundred in total) that dynamically appeared based on the page and how the customer got to the site, so that when customers called a certain number, it would be obvious where they encountered problems. Hotels.com used these capabilities to identify problems that would otherwise have escaped notice.

The real cultural shift happened as the result of an early, big find. Megibow discovered that a large percentage of customers who had made it all the way to the end of the checkout process did not complete a transaction. It turned out that a combination of unclear messaging, user flows, database issues, and outright bugs may have caused the majority of these customers to abandon the process, although they probably intended to complete a transaction. Based on these results, the GM of Hotels.com supported reprioritizing projects, bringing all relevant groups to the table and operating at an above-normal pace. In a matter of days, all of the problems were solved. Not only did the change bring immediate additional revenue, but it showed the team how analytics, when used collaboratively across the company, could drive tangible improvements for customers and for the internal operations of the company. This "site conversion" cross-functional team continued to meet twice weekly for almost two years. As of this writing, hundreds of additional opportunities have been discovered.

Megibow reports that by removing obstacles and providing insights into better site design, Hotels.com has substantially improved its conversion rate—the percentage of Web site customers who actually book rooms. The company has also created "tons of customer goodwill" by solving their Web site problems. Finally, he says, they are winning in the shift to a more customer-focused culture. It couldn't have been done, however, without a strong analytical culture for support. Megibow has moved to the Expedia organization now, and is attempting to establish the same culture of using analysis to root out and fix problems.

Other Cultural Attributes of Analytical Firms

Certain cultural attributes help to reinforce an analytical culture. In effect, well-managed organizations with clearly defined cultures will be more likely to adopt an analytical orientation.

Transparency in an organization's culture encourages an analytical orientation. Not surprisingly, the willingness to freely share facts about the business is akin to appreciating these facts. As Warren Bennis, Dan Goleman, and Pat Biederman have noted in their book *Transparency*:

> An organization's capacity to compete, solve problems, innovate, meet challenges, and achieve goals—its intelligence, if you will—varies to the degree that the flow of information remains healthy. That is particularly true when the information in question consists of crucial but hard-to-take facts, the information that leaders may bristle at hearing—and that subordinates too often, and understandably, play down, disguise, or ignore. For information to flow freely within an institution, followers must feel free to speak openly, and leaders must welcome such openness.[4]

Sharing this "flow of information" is particularly important for analytical cultures. If you don't care about data and analysis and their power to transform an organization, you are not likely to spread them broadly. On the other hand, firms that are highly analytical will want employees, and maybe even Wall Street analysts and shareholders, to know about the data and analysis, particularly if they shed a positive light on the business.

Other cultural strengths can also be translated to analytical strengths. For example, the *pay for performance* culture, a close relative of transparency, creates a demand for performance metrics and motivates managers and employees to attend to them. Similarly, a culture that believes in infrastructure and process management will facilitate the generation of information and respond to operational problems that analytics point out. Finally, a culture that clearly communicates strategic direction will make it much easier to determine where analytics should be applied to the business.

Truly analytical firms not only gather data and analyze it; they also use it to *make tough calls and carry out tough actions*. They don't allow experience, industry tradition, sentimental attachment, or nagging voices in their heads to create inertia; if the numbers suggest that something isn't working, they stop doing it.

For example, a customer orientation entails separating the best customers from the worst and "firing" the customers who lose money for the organization. Similarly, analytical cultures must make tough decisions like discontinuing products that don't make money or letting go of unproductive employees. Barry Beracha, the former CEO of Earthgrains (now a part of Sara Lee), is one of our analytical heroes because he used data to fire bad customers and products, thereby initiating a dramatic turnaround at his company.[5]

Recognizing the Roadblocks

Firms with an analytical culture don't keep up time-honored activities just because they're time-honored. We talked with one consumer products firm, for example, that uses a lot of analytics but hasn't established an analytical culture. As a market researcher explained, "We buy tons of data on the consumer products market. We analyze the hell out of it. The problem is, we don't change anything as a result of it." He went on to describe the results of a marketing mix portfolio analysis that determined which marketing programs were most effective: "We figured out that a lot of our television advertising wasn't that effective. But I don't think we've decreased it at all." The leaders of the marketing function, he explained, either didn't believe the analysis or weren't comfortable with the implications.

Similarly, one retailer that is trying to progress in an analytical direction has hit a cultural roadblock. The company has a successful loyalty program that generates vast amounts of data that the company uses to tailor promotions to customers. However, because the marketing organization is structured by product categories, each category manager acts in the best interest of his or her category but often hurts store performance overall. They have a pool of money to offer customers, but category managers want to use it in their own areas, ignoring overall profitability. Judicious manipulation of organizational structure and incentives might fix the retailer's fragmented approach, but so far it hasn't.

Another problem at this retailer is an irrational attachment to circulars—those weekly ads inserted in your Sunday newspaper. Circulars have been around forever, but for this retailer, there is precious little evidence that they are effective as a marketing tool. Nobody knows who reads them, or whose shopping behavior they influence. Yet, despite the distinct possibility that these inserts are more commonly used as birdcage liners, the head of advertising at the company continues to spend money on them.

Such inertia is common in business generally, but analytical cultures minimize it. Instead, they are resolute that data and analytics will drive action. If something no longer makes sense—even if it's been done that way for eons—they find the courage to stop doing it. In short, organizations with analytical cultures make analytical decisions a high priority and recognize their value.

A financial services organization we've worked with has encountered different roadblocks. The company has brought us in several times to speak to middle managers about analytical competition. They always seem to get our message, but each time we ask "Who's going to take these ideas to Bob," the company's imposing CEO, no one ever raises a hand.

The company has a centralized group for customer analytics, but it isn't well integrated with the rest of the organization—or even with the marketing function. A number of analytical studies are undertaken, but always piecemeal and in silos—so there is no way to get a unified perspective on the customer. One senior analyst described the problem:

> We think we are an analytical culture, but we think we're better than we are. We have analytical overconfidence. We get stuck in the same practices and methods. Sometimes we do go deeper and deeper in one area, but then it gets harder to link across all the little silos. We never get the true power of linking the information together. Analytics people are

treated as a specialty function—not embedded in the business. Managers effectively say, "Thanks for the information and hopefully it will support the case I'm making." Analytics are a black box and the group that does them is a black box. Our CEO doesn't know the true power of analytical decision making. And most managers are not open to hearing things they don't expect or believe. We set up an entire framework to measure marketing effectiveness. We measured it all. Then marketing did what they always did. They think they're doing it all right, but they need more insecurity. Having the capability isn't the same thing as doing something with it.

Despite its shortcomings, the company was doing well, at least until the current financial crisis. Now that it's struggling, it has cut out several people from the analytics group. In this company analytics are viewed as just another business activity—useful, but not essential, to decision makers.

Building Your Analytical Culture

Of course, you can't build analytical culture everywhere in your organization. The specific places where you do establish it (or first establish it) should be:

- Endowed with a great deal of data that isn't being sufficiently analyzed today.

- Important to your business success.

- Led by a manager who already understands the importance of analytics.

- Blessed with a cadre of people who have some analytical skills.

For example, analyzing Web data and metrics is a good place to begin building an analytical culture because the data is rich, the people involved are typically young and technology focused, and the Web is an increasingly important customer channel for most organizations.[6] It's also a fairly recent development in business, so for many organizations, the state of Web analytics is primitive relative to what's possible.

Having an analytical culture provides notice that "how we do things around here" includes making decisions on the basis of data, facts, and rigorous analysis. Getting to this point isn't quick or easy, but once you're there, it's a competitive advantage. Progressive Insurance, for example, knows that most competitors won't be able to institute a strong analytical orientation overnight. One executive there commented to us in an interview:

> We've been doing analytics for quite a while, and it's baked into our culture. A nonanalytical culture is very hard to change—you'd have to overcome senior managers who base big decisions on intuition. Plus we have really deep bench strength—senior managers have had experience in many different areas, and they're comfortable with how data-based decisions are used in all of them. Even if you put in a new department of analytical people, you can't change a culture by creating a department.

Of course, even with their strong analytical cultures, leaders like Progressive can never rest on their laurels. They must come up with new strategies, new data, new models, and new analytical technologies if they want to stay ahead of competitors. The analytical organizations of the future will be those in which analytical cultures as well as capabilities are actively renewed and redeveloped over time. Not coincidentally, how to do that is the subject of the next chapter.

9

REVIEW YOUR BUSINESS COMPREHENSIVELY

BEING ANALYTICAL—or more specifically, being successful with analytics—is not a one-time activity. Analytical competitors must constantly review and revise their approaches in light of their business strategies and business models, changing market conditions, competitor initiatives, and the expectations and behaviors of customers. These days the world changes rapidly and analytical models need to reflect the changes. In this chapter, we discuss how to keep track of your analytical processes and models to make it easier to stay in sync with changing business conditions.

The 2007–2009 financial crisis provides an excellent illustration of the importance of continuous review of analytics. Financial institutions repeatedly failed to undertake timely reviews of their financial models and assumptions. When housing prices stopped rising in 2006, customers' ability to pay off mortgages through refinancing was no longer possible, but banks continued to make subprime loans. The banks simply didn't monitor and revise their analytical models closely enough.

In an industry like financial services where effective analytics are key to success, firms need to continually review analytical models, assumptions, and management frameworks. These activities are not just good management hygiene; they are a means to survival.

Constant Review to Create New Insights

One important aspect of analytical review is never resting on your laurels. Eternal vigilance is needed to seek out new insights and stay a step (or two or three) ahead of the competition. Progressive Insurance, the third-largest auto insurance firm in the United States, has consistently reviewed its analytical orientation and developed new offerings over time. The company pioneered or adopted early several analytical innovations in the automobile insurance industry, including segmenting high-risk drivers (some had higher risks than others—called "nonstandard" risk), establishing many different price points by risk level, rating drivers based in part on their credit scores and behaviors, and gathering information on actual driver behavior ("pay as you drive") through its MyRate program. Progressive was rewarded for its innovations by a high rate of growth relative to competitors.

However, in most cases, competitors adopted the same approaches—usually a few years after Progressive did. Allstate, for example, hired an architect of Progressive's credit scoring approach to implement a similar program, and eventually moved from three different price points to four hundred.[1] A 2001 survey found that 92 percent of property and casualty insurance firms were using credit scores and other measures of financial responsibility for underwriting new policies, and Progressive had only adopted this practice broadly in 1996.[2] It's relatively easy to copy innovations in the insurance industry, because carriers must file documents with state insurance commissions on how they price and operate. That doesn't give you everything you need to copy an analytical innovation, but it provides a start.

So Progressive must keep coming up with new ideas. One of the company's executives suggested that it does so through multiple means:[3]

- It has a strong measurement-oriented culture; virtually everything possible is measured.

- It hires and retains people who have an analytical orientation plus a detailed understanding of the business.

- It ensures that any innovations draw heavily on the company's long data history (Progressive has been in business since 1937).

Most important, analytical innovations at Progressive comple-ment its other strategic advantages. The company has focused on several different strategic capabilities in addition to analytics: a direct-to-consumer competency to augment its industry-leading distribu-tion through independent agents, a strong brand, convenient and efficient claims processing, and the use of the Internet as a channel to customers. When considering new analytical offerings, Progressive also considers how they might interact with other strategic orienta-tions. For example, its initiative to provide consumers with compara-tive pricing information (Progressive's price compared to its estimate of competitors' prices) combined well with the ability to provide prices over the Internet. Sources outside of Progressive suggest that the company probably also maintains an advantage in the extent and complexity of its data and analyses. In pricing, for example, one study found that in one of the markets it serves, Progressive employed over a billion different pricing "cells" (variables times the number of cate-gories per variable). The next closest competitor had one-tenth as many cells.[4]

Reviewing Strategy and Business Models

When analytics are used in support of particular strategies and business models, their role needs to be continually reviewed and updated. Ana-lytics make it possible to optimize a strategy, but they are of little value if the strategy itself is no longer viable. Careful monitoring makes organi-zations more adroit at knowing when it is time to shift strategies. Two organizations that we'll discuss in this context are Capital One, which has changed its strategy and business model, and American Airlines, which hasn't yet but probably should.

If you've read *Competing on Analytics*, or if you've watched TV or re-ceived mail in the United States lately, you've heard of Capital One. The company is among the most analytical of firms, and until recently, the most successful. It was founded as a business unit of Signet Bank, and from its spinoff in 1994 up through 2004, it grew earnings per share and return on equity by over 20 percent every year. But by 2005, Capital One's executives seemed to realize that its primary business—con-sumer credit cards—was not sufficient to ensure continued success. To avoid being acquired by other banks and to ensure a source of low-cost deposits, it needed to become a full-fledged bank. It therefore bought Hibernia Bank in Louisiana, North Fork Bank in New York, and Chevy Chase Bank in Virginia.

After these acquisitions, Capital One needed to figure out how its "information-based strategy" worked in the new banking business. Its managers immediately set about translating their ethos into the full-service banking context, which required new data, new models, and new assumptions. As one employee told us, "It's much easier to do randomized testing with direct-mail envelopes than with branch bankers." We believe that an innovative firm like Capital One will ultimately figure out how to be an analytical competitor in its current business environment, but it's not going to happen overnight.

American Airlines was another early analytical competitor, and was earlier at it than almost any other firm. It started its analytical approach to "yield management," or optimized pricing, in 1985. This approach helped to put some upstart competitors (including People Express) out of business, and according to an operations research society (IN-FORMS), its yield management systems contributed $1.4 billion in a three-year period at the airline.[5] Today, however, virtually every airline has yield management capabilities, some having learned it from American's consulting organization, so optimized pricing no longer provides any competitive advantage.

American also uses analytics to optimize its route network and crew schedules. Without analytical tools, managing a complex hub-and-spoke network with over 250 destinations, twelve aircraft types, and 3,400 daily flights would be nearly impossible. Nevertheless, it might be argued that American's optimized complexity works against it. Neither it nor other major U.S. airlines with similar complexity levels have been very profitable for years.

A much less complex airline model is offered by Southwest Airlines, which has only one aircraft type and no airport hubs. Southwest also uses analytics for seat pricing and operations, but its model is much simpler to optimize. Most important, Southwest has been profitable for thirty-six consecutive years, and at several times over the recent past its market value has been worth more than the combined market value of all other U.S. carriers. This sobering comparison suggests that American and the other more complex carriers need to simplify their own business models.

Reviewing Analytical Targets

We argued in chapter 5 that analytical targets are important, and that they should be driven by your organization's strategy and business models. If those change—and they should as the world changes—then the analytical targets should change as well. At a global retail finance organization, for example, the need for a "target review" became very apparent when the head of analytics met with some of his internal customers in the U.K. "We are grateful for the mortgage and lending models you have provided for us," he was told, "However, they are all wrong and need to be made much more conservative." Further remarks led to the change in targets: "In addition, we would like you to change your focus entirely going forward to concentrate on risk—credit risk, asset management risk, enterprise risk, you name it."

Now, as the analytics manager noted in a discussion with us, a wholesale shift from credit to risk analytics wouldn't necessarily be wise. Financial institutions need a balance of focus on risk and opportunity. But you can bet that he and his group are now pursuing risk analytics in a much more aggressive way.

We've seen changes in analytical targets in the retail industry that were also motivated by difficult economic times. Several companies in that industry were pursuing analytical strategies based on loyalty programs and customer intelligence. Their primary focus was on how to get currently loyal customers to buy more. Since the economic downturn began in 2008, several retailers have shifted their primary target for analytical work to cost reduction and efficient marketing. One, for example, is focusing on marketing mix optimization topics. A company executive we interviewed admitted, "We're trying to figure out, at long last, whether our advertising circulars really work, and are comparing them to more targeted offers." Another retailer that primarily addresses customers through catalogs is pruning its mailing list to those customers who have responded with profitable purchases over the last two years. It is also customizing the content of the catalogs by sending longer, heavier catalogs to better customers. Though these practices may seem like punishing loyal buyers with more and bulkier junk mail, both marketing mix optimization and targeted mailings can save considerable amounts in marketing budgets. Another retailer sought to improve profitability by minimizing returns. Whereas the previous focus had been on identifying the best customers, the company began to identify attributes of "serial returners"—customers who routinely return items—and then took steps to reduce the offers they received. The retailer also retrained the sales force to make certain that customers were happy with their potential purchases before the sale.

Reviewing Competitors

It's also important to constantly review the analytical activities of competitors to understand how your own activities compare to theirs. You may believe you have a lead, but competitors can catch up—particularly if they have the same sources of data. Meanwhile, your competitors may have adopted analytical approaches that you should be emulating. Of course, if you hope to get any sort of competitive advantage from your analytical activities, just emulating your competitors won't get you very far.

A systematic approach to assessing competitors is likely to yield the greatest benefit. The model in figure 9-1 illustrates the competitive analysis undertaken by a firm in the health care industry.

FIGURE 9-1

Competitive analytics capability model

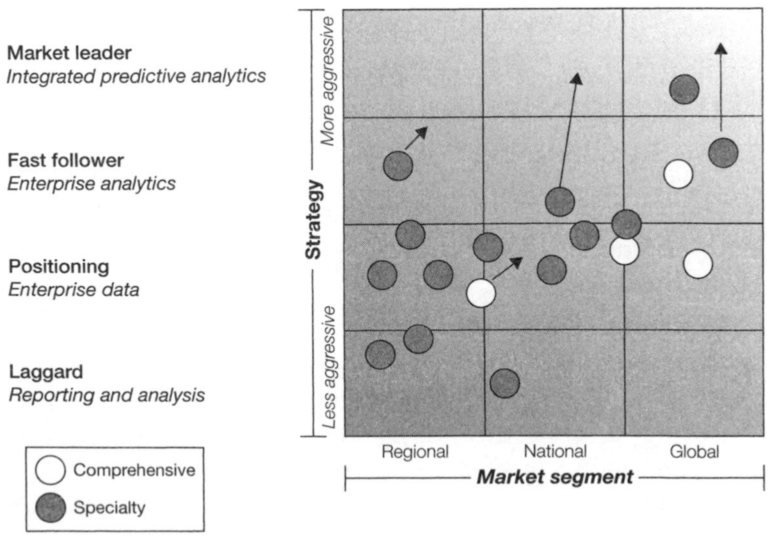

The bubbles represent each competitor's current market position and strategy vis-a-vis analytics; the arrow depicts the competitor's future direction. The shades of gray represent different types of competitors. For each market segment or product line, the framework assesses the key characteristics of analytical investments and the strategic objective of their analytical capabilities. These will vary by industry; the health care firm defined four levels:

- *Laggards: Reporting and analysis.* The company has limited interest in analytics beyond traditional reporting of data. It is waiting for further proof of adoption for evidence-based medicine before investing in analytics. It may be exploring options for business intelligence products, tools, and programs. (Though if our suspicions are correct, it may not survive long enough to see these initiatives through.)

- *Positioning for analytics: Enterprise data.* The company recognizes there is a significant risk of diminished market share and adverse selection because of deficiencies in their analytical capabilities. It makes investments in IT and people to support internal analytical needs. It is upgrading information and IT applications to provide a basis for better analytics.

- *Fast followers: Enterprise analytics.* The company views business intelligence and informatics as part of its "competency portfolio" and acknowledges that analytics could become a force for transformational change in the industry. It makes significant investments in new and upgraded analytical capabilities.

- *Market leaders: Integrated predictive analytics.* The company views analytics as a growth engine and a high priority for investment. It aggressively acquires information assets and competencies. It makes the development of unique and proprietary data a priority. Management is committed to transforming the company through the use of predictive analytics. The company offers new, analytically based products and services to differentiate from competitors.

We're not advocating "analytical espionage," but getting competitive intelligence about analytical projects and capabilities is usually a fairly straightforward task. You can talk with industry consultants or academics, interview or hire analytical people who have worked for competitors, view job opening descriptions, attend conferences, and so forth. And, of course, you will observe competitors' behavior in the marketplace. Investing in a high-powered telescope is probably a last resort.

One of the best examples of analytics and competition is the transformation of the Oakland A's described in the book *Moneyball* by Michael Lewis.[6] When selecting players, the team moved from focusing on players' intangible attributes to their actual past performance. One metric they employed earlier than other teams was "on-base percentage," which includes both walks and hits—whereas the primary metric of the past, batting average, includes only hits. Of course, it wasn't very difficult for other teams to find out what Oakland was up to. If they couldn't figure it out from their draft choices, they could eventually read about it in a best-selling book. Not surprisingly, our sources in professional baseball say that on-base percentage is now overvalued in the market for talent. As two economists who studied the issue put it (in somewhat academic jargon): "Our tests provided econometric support for Lewis' claim of mis-pricing in the baseball labor market's valuation of batting skills. We also found suggestive evidence that the dispersion of statistical knowledge throughout baseball organizations was associated with a sharp attenuation of the mis-pricing."[7]

So what is a smart baseball team to do? There is really only one answer: keep on developing new analytics. That's why the Boston Red Sox hired a crack baseball statistician like Bill James. He's come up with dozens of ways to measure player and team performance (and he's much better at keeping secrets). Similarly, companies have to keep innovating in ways that are consistent with their strategies and business models.

In addition to assessing how well you are competing with analytics against other companies, you should also review the benefits of collaborating with them. Collaboration has been particularly effective in health insurance, where nineteen different Blue Cross and Blue Shield organizations around the United States have banded together to sponsor the Blue Health Intelligence (BHI) initiative at the Blue Cross and Blue Shield Association. The plans have furnished claims data (with no personal identification) on 79 million members. Health care provider and pharmacy data are also being added to the database. The large scale of the database allows not only benchmarking comparisons across state and regional plans, but also analytical projects that can be generalized to a national population. BHI analysts, for example, are studying pediatric diabetes patients and trying to predict the occurrence of hospitalizations. They're also assessing whether spinal surgeries actually reduce back pain. Only by combining forces could BHI get enough data to perform such analyses.

Reviewing Customers and Partners

Customers and their preferences can change over time, so it's important to ensure that any models based on customer opportunity, risk, or behavior are reviewed frequently. At Netflix, for example, many of the behavioral models for customers were created when the company was founded around the turn of the twenty-first century. Those customers were relative pioneers in ordering movies online. By the middle of the decade, however, Netflix analysts began to question whether the typical customer was very different from that in 2000. Certainly they were no longer pioneers. So the analysts began to retest their models. Without retesting, the models would probably not fit the data for these new customers.

A major Canadian bank conducts frequent customer reviews to gauge their customers' willingness to supply information to and be contacted by the bank. This particular bank relies on customer contacts to supply new relationships; it offers preferred pricing not only to good customers, but to their relatives and sometimes even close business associates. The bank also uses "event triggers" (e.g., a major cash deposit) to predict when the customer might value an interaction with the bank. The bank's customer information managers check several times a year the percentage of customers who request "Do not call" status. Fortunately for the bank, the percentage has remained at about 5 percent for many years—must be that legendary Canadian neighborliness. However, the bank also buys lists of potential customers from external data providers, and on the lists they buy, 50 percent are on the "Do not call" list. As a result of this review, the bank is considering no longer purchasing external lists.

Companies should also review their "analytical ecosystems" to determine whether they have the right partners. In the retail industry, for example, a retailer can create its own analytics. It can also supplement those with analytics from data providers such as Nielsen and Information

Resources, from real-time promotions vendors such as Catalina, from consumer products suppliers, from analytical consultants (onshore and offshore), and from vendors of analytical software and hardware. If for some reason the internal analytical resources aren't up to the task, there are many possible alternatives.

Reviewing Technology, Data, and Information

Firms should also review at least annually the new technologies and information that might affect their businesses in the future. For example, it seems quite likely that retail and distribution businesses will have massive amounts of data available when RFID (radio frequency identification) and electronic product code (EPC) devices become widely available. These were predicted to arrive at reasonable cost several years ago—Wal-Mart required them of suppliers on a pilot basis in 2005, then backed away from the requirement—but their eventual arrival seems inevitable.

Firms that care about competitive advantage from supply chain analytics should be thinking now about how they will factor all the available data into their analytical decisions and how systems and processes will take advantage of the analytics. With products broadcasting their identity, it will be much easier to know what's on store shelves, and hence much easier to create and update demand forecasts, replenishment models, and logistical optimization models. Not all of the detailed work to accommodate these technologies should be done today, but some planning should begin now.

Similarly, firms in industries where electrical energy is generated, distributed, or consumed in large amounts will soon be blessed with large amounts of data for energy management. In the "smart grids" of the future, devices that use or meter energy will broadcast their energy use for centralized monitoring and management. Devices that distribute energy will be able to provide not only energy consumption information but also details of cost and carbon creation. Analytics will be needed to make intelligent decisions about how to use energy wisely and how to deploy it across organizations. Anyone involved in the energy industry should be thinking now about how to analyze and use this new data.

Other industries already have data-intensive technologies in place, but only in a limited number of their sectors. As the technologies become more pervasive, considerable opportunities for analytical exploitation will arise. In health care, for example, if U.S. providers can ever standardize electronic medical records, very large amounts of data will become available for analysis. With sufficient analytics, providers and payers will develop a greater understanding of which treatments are effective and which patients might benefit from disease management approaches. A few leading institutions are already doing some of this analysis, but every organization in the industry should be planning for it.

In short, with new data sources from the Internet and information providers appearing daily, you should be reviewing the role that analytical decisions might play in your future. The companies that are very capable with analytics didn't get that way by always reacting to problems and opportunities—they anticipated and prepared for them.

Reviewing and Managing Models

"Model management," the systematic process of creating, monitoring, and deploying analytical models, helps a company constantly review its use of analytics in its interactions with the outside world. There are plenty of reasons to review and manage your models:

- Knowing what models you have in place—as well as what data they use, what assumptions they make, and how and by whom they were created—makes it much easier to find and change them when necessary.

- Keeping track of all of the competing models allows you to know which ones are winning (in the process of developing models, there are many "challengers" and eventually a single "champion").

- Keeping track of the multiple versions of your model (which, like any computer code, can have many variations) is important.

- You can check to see how well a particular model is working and alert analysts to "model decay." If the world changes, for example, if mortgage recipients can no longer pay off their loans, a model decay analysis would suggest a change in credit issuance models, signifying that models and their underlying assumptions need updating.

- Regulatory requirements of certain industries, like banking, mandate some degree of model management (although we admit they didn't seem to help much in preventing the financial crisis).

Despite these virtues, effective model management should go beyond regulatory requirements and internal control documentation. Effective model management and analytics can be used as a competitive advantage. Coordinating models for assessing accounts, transactions, products, business lines, and risk factors help to optimize business decisions. Going further to align accounting valuation models helps to capture the effectiveness of business performance while reducing the noise and burden of variances. For instance, Capital One went beyond directives from federal regulators and embarked upon a systematic effort to capture and document its analytical models. They realized how coordinating internal models and analytics could be used to better model customer behavior and roll up to overall business line and company performance. Other large banks, including CitiGroup, State Street, and JPMorgan Chase have recognized the value of analytical models involving different asset types and have created centralized model libraries and teams of experts to support business lines and ensure diligence in the application of models. Such teams are typically referred to in terms of "model validation" and are normally found in risk management functions.

As organizations become increasingly reliant on their analytical models, we bet that more and more will realize how important model management is. For an increasing number of firms, their analytical models are their gold mines, their oil reservoirs, their bank deposits. To keep track of them and pay attention to how well they're working is only common sense.

Analytical leaders—firms and managers that are ahead of the pack in analytical orientation—recognize that the business environment for any firm changes rapidly, and to be successful, their analytical orientation must change with it. In industries where analytics have been broadly adopted—from banking to baseball—review is the only way for an organization to stay on top. It is the antidote to the "resting on their laurels" syndrome that otherwise takes leaders into a period of slow decline.

10

MEETING CHALLENGES
ALONG THE WAY

IN 2006, COO Shawn Ket brought a new focus on analytics to Credit-Corp, a Sydney, Australia–based company specializing in acquiring and managing consumer debt. The company has grown rapidly, with revenue increasing at least 60 percent per year between 2003 and 2008. He established an analytics group that utilizes the largest distressed debt database in Australia for pricing, customer acquisition, and identification of potential customers in a positive financial turnaround. The group also analyzes workflows in debt management operations and handles many ad hoc inquiries for analytics from around the company. Jolie Baasch, the group's head, describes the company's rapid transition toward analytics. "Six to eight months ago it seemed that all decisions were made on intuition—now all are being made on analytics."[1] However, that fast increase in demand created far more work than Baasch's eight-person group could handle. What to do next?

Trying to build up capability to meet exploding demand when analytical talent is scarce is one of four challenges and transition points we discuss in this chapter:

- Building initial momentum for analytical initiatives.

- Organizing to manage analytics when senior management gets serious.

- Expanding capacity when analytics takes off.

- Driving to become an analytical enterprise.

In part 1 (and the appendix) we discuss building the capabilities to put important analytical applications in place. In this chapter, however, we look at the journey from more of a supply-and-demand perspective. How do you build the business appetite for analytics, satisfy that appetite, and encourage a healthy analytical diet across the enterprise?

Gaining Momentum for Analytics

Learning to improve business performance through analytics is not a precise science—ironically, it's not yet very analytical. You've got to find the formula that unlocks interest in your organization. You have to figure out what motivates leaders and understand the formula that creates interest in applying analytics to business problems and opportunities. In addition to being DELTA-ready, you need to find the ways to build momentum. Here are three common scenarios:

- *A well-defined business problem, performance shortfall, or explicit improvement opportunity lends itself to analytics.* The target may be clear, but management motivation may not be high enough if the problem is owned by functional managers. You may need to elevate sponsorship, especially if the analytical solution will be cross-functional. So focus on leadership and be otherwise DELTA-ready when you get the go-ahead.

- *A key executive recognizes that the business is neglecting a hoard of potentially valuable data associated with a business process* (e.g., point-of-sale data, claims history, employee experience). In this scenario, uncover the data's specific potential for process improvement and get someone in top management to recognize the business value of exploiting it. Make sure that the data is truly ready and that you have a specific target, not a vague charter.

- *Top management recognizes that a strategic business opportunity, one that's important to business performance and growth, depends on analytics.* Often just an intuition, this realization may seem like the ideal scenario for generating momentum; however, any delay may frustrate management's expectations and have the opposite effect. Delay is common when the opportunity needs further definition and qualification and other DELTA elements (especially data and analysts) are not ready. Be realistic about your readiness, skilled at managing the expectations of senior management, and ambitious to succeed.

Note that all three scenarios center on specific applications and targets, not on encouraging the organization at large to work more analytically. That comes later. Even if your CEO or COO is a real "data dog," pushing for more analytical management across the corporation, you'll still need to build momentum one application and one decision at a time. The key player is the executive responsible for the business problem or opportunity being addressed. Also note that you'll likely have to build momentum in different parts of the business at different times and in different ways, so this isn't a once-and-done exercise.

Table 10-1 summarizes these three scenarios. Yours will be different, but it may well be a variation on one of these. The key lesson here is

TABLE 10-1

Gaining momentum for analytics

Scenario	Situation	Who cares?
We have a problem or improvement opportunity.	• Need to raise performance, perhaps in response to a competitor • Need to lower cost, improve asset utilization, or change cost structure • Need to increase innovation or accelerate time to market	Mid to upper functional management, making targeting easier than investing
We have a data hoard.	• Have an accumulation of potentially useful data that has yet to be explored and exploited • Ideally use in combination with other assets—analysts and technology	Who recognizes the potential? CIOs are often early sponsors; helps if top management includes some "data dogs"
We have a strategic opportunity.	• Determined to compete on a different basis, to solve a problem nobody else has mastered, to be the best at something important • Determined to invest to seize the opportunity	Top management, which puts the pressure on, especially if the assets aren't ready

to look not only at your DELTA readiness, but also at how analytics can and should play out in your business.

Organizing to Manage Analytics

When top management begins to get serious about analytics and adopt an enterprise perspective on resources and applications priorities, it's time to conduct a formal assessment of your analytical capabilities, create a management structure to guide analytical initiatives, and develop a business strategy for analytics. The DELTA model provides a means for thorough assessment of your analytical capabilities. But how to organize and develop strategy is very company-specific. Health-care insurer Humana provides a good example of how to proceed.

Since 2001, Humana has grown from a regional health care payer to one of the country's largest health insurers, providing health plans and prescription drugs to more than 18 million members. Meanwhile, changing market conditions have been shifting the entire industry toward a more analytical management style. Evidence-based medicine promised a statistically based approach to more cost-effective treatments and better health for patients. Informatics (health care jargon for data-based analytics) was becoming central to Humana's ability to serve its customers and manage costs.[2]

As an early adopter of an enterprise data warehouse, Humana faced several common pitfalls, such as weak integration between business and IT objectives and inadequate policies regarding the governance of enterprise data. In addition, various functional silos of analytics were making it difficult both to leverage data and to maintain and upgrade the enterprise data warehouse.

Jim Murray, Humana's COO, emphasized the importance of taking an enterprisewide approach to analytics that would "eliminate silos of analytics and facilitate the flow of trusted, consistent and accurate information to all of Humana."[3] Toward that end, Humana established a new position to lead analytics—vice president, Humana Integrated Informatics—and recruited Lisa Tourville, an experienced actuarial consultant, for this crucial role.

Recognizing the importance of top management leadership, Tourville assembled a team of business and IT leaders to develop

Humana's analytical strategy, which went under the name "business intelligence and informatics." The steering committee included Jim Murray; Jim Bloem, chief financial officer; Steve McCulley, Humana's corporate controller; Brian LeClaire, chief technology officer; and Bruce Goodman, chief service and information officer. The team's business objectives were significant: to assess the company's readiness for an analytical transformation throughout Humana's organization, processes, and systems; to develop an industry-leading analytical strategy; to connect analytics to the company's business strategy; and improve the return on current analytical investments.

With sponsorship from the executive suite, the team concluded that Humana needed to build an analytical "competency center" in order to integrate decentralized business units with the corporate team that builds and maintains the data warehouse. This center would also perform the critical role of champion of business intelligence and analytics for Humana. A steering committee would oversee the center in order to ensure that its work stayed aligned with Humana's strategic objectives.

Tourville and the team then devised a road map for Humana that included priorities to expand analytical capabilities and build the foundation for a more analytical enterprise. First, the team assessed the data and the enterprise IT capabilities needed to support analytical activities, and in the process helped the businesses to become better at articulating business requirements for new data sources and analytics. Second, it helped Humana take an enterprisewide approach to prioritizing its investments (human, technical, and operational) in analytics. Third, it identified industry-specific opportunities to apply analytics in high-value ways. Fourth, it made sure executives recognized the importance of their roles as leaders of analytical initiatives and role models for an analytical mind-set. Finally, the team developed recommendations for identifying, developing, and rewarding analytical talent.

From this assessment and plan, Humana gained a deep understanding of the human performance and the technological and operational challenges underpinning the company's expanding use of analytics. As a more analytical organization, Humana is now better equipped to facilitate profitable growth, to develop and manage cutting-edge products and services, to build trusted relationships, and to educate member communities on how to improve their physical and economic health.

When Demand Exceeds Supply

Let's return to the case of CreditCorp. We left them in the common predicament of finding that demand for analytics has suddenly outstripped the capacity of the analyst group to provide services. In analytical companies, this increased demand comes in waves when different parts of the business get excited about the potential of analytics. It's difficult to be 100 percent prepared to ramp up because demand can grow very quickly, and few corporations (especially in recessionary times) will invest in overbuilding analytical capacity in advance of that demand. So you need to anticipate by having resources (starting with data) as ready as possible, preparing to act when the time comes, and knowing that no single action is going to do the trick.

At CreditCorp, Jolie Baasch and her analysts deal with increasing demand through multiple approaches. Analysts try to encourage frontline staff to do the analytics themselves (to the degree possible) through education programs and distribution of the information necessary to make analytical decisions. In some cases, the analysts can identify the business drivers, and then the users of the application can monitor them and see how they change over time. They also build reusable production applications—not "one-offs." But the biggest lever in managing demand and prioritizing efforts is clarity about the strategic issues of the business. Baasch holds regular discussions with the COO and the head of business services to keep current on what's important to Credit-Corp. Before undertaking a project, the analysts determine how long it will take to solve the problem and discuss priorities and time frames with the customer.

Imbalance of supply and demand may seem to arise quickly, but beneath the surface it is driven by a combination of factors over time:

- Analysts, especially those we've termed "analytical pros," may be in short supply—difficult to find, recruit, and retain.

- Demand can grow rapidly once a business gets a taste of analytics and notable applications succeed. Sometimes the demand is pent up awaiting better data, then unleashed in a torrent as the data becomes available (as at CreditCorp).

- Supply can be wasted on the wrong things, so business opportunities for analytics are missed. This happens when opportunities and priorities are not clear, when analysts work in local silos and can't collaborate on strategic enterprise initiatives, and when analysts spend too much time generating reports (work that analytical amateurs should be able to do for themselves) rather than building and maintaining models.

What do you do when supply exceeds demand? No, college undergrads in Intro to Economics classes, the answer is not "lower prices." As CreditCorp shows, it takes a set of actions to increase supply and, ideally, to keep building it in concert with demand. Figure 10-1 depicts the situation where total demand for analytics is larger than available supply, and only part of the demand is of high business value. The numbered arrows represent three sets of possible tactics for bringing supply and demand into better alignment: increasing the supply of analysts, managing the level of demand, and increasing the quality of demand.

To *increase the supply of analysts* and analytics services, an enterprise can:

- Hire more analysts (though competition for the best may be fierce).

- Outsource selected analytics projects and services.

- Improve the work methods of analysts to increase their productivity, usually with an emphasis on reuse of templates and models.

- Improve the data and technology infrastructure for analytics so that all projects can be delivered more productively.

- Partner with like-minded business improvement groups such as Six Sigma or business process reengineering, that are

FIGURE 10-1

Aligning supply and demand

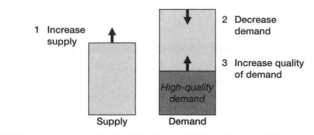

working analytically and cross-functionally, as a means of expanding capability and focusing on high-value enterprise projects.

Demand management is an important activity in any services organization. We don't want to stifle the business's appetite for analytics, but we do want to mitigate that portion of demand that must be filled by the analyst group, especially when there are alternative ways of meeting it. To *manage demand*, an enterprise can:

- Train more analytical amateurs to meet their own needs for straightforward analyses and reports.

- Improve the evaluation and prioritization of projects, preferably with an enterprise perspective and perhaps through a program management office, to reduce low-value demand.

- Negotiate and plan demand levels with customer management as part of the process of educating them on how best to make use of analytics.

- Negotiate with customer management about "information sufficiency"—how complete and accurate the data really needs to be for analytics to be useful.

To *increase the quality of demand*, an organization can:

- Educate customer executives and the corporate leadership team on how to maximize the business value of analytics, including the roles of smart demand and capable supply.

- Perform strategic, enterprisewide evaluation and prioritization of analytics projects.

- Apply portfolio management to the set of analytics projects, continuously evaluating the progress and value of individual projects and the overall mix.

- Consult regularly with customer management on the quality of their demand for analytics and the business value that they are generating.

- Suggest to customer management opportunities for high-value application of analytics.

Like CreditCorp, many companies we studied employ combinations of these tactics. The right approach depends on the analytical experience and orientation of the corporation and its business units, as well as constraints like funding. But especially as a business unit is becoming familiar with business analytics, the leaders of analyst organizations must educate and shape business demand so that analysts are free to work on the most strategic and value-adding business applications. Here are three examples.

A *hospitality company* was analytically sophisticated in its customer/revenue operations. Other business functions began noticing and increasing their demand for analytics. Already stretched thin, analysts were dispersed across the company. The company responded with three main thrusts: invest in enterprise data and infrastructure for analytics to provide a better platform for the growing portfolio of applications, develop "template models" for rapid reuse in similar applications, and establish informal centers of expertise for experience-sharing among analysts working in major business areas.

An *energy company* had gotten ahead of the competition in important areas like customer service and wanted to leverage analytics to maintain its lead, but too much of its analyst capacity was devoted to predictable and time-consuming analyses for rate cases and regulatory requirements. The leaders of the analyst group partnered with the VP of corporate strategy to make competitive applications a priority. They divided the project portfolio into categories—major/competitive, regulatory/ongoing, and ad hoc—and focused on managing the level of each in the overall mix. They also consulted more actively with their business counterparts on information sufficiency and negotiated major project attributes (functionality, timing, cost), not all of which could be maximized.

A *consumer goods company's* success with analytics in supply chain applications, coupled with a new corporate focus on profitability analysis, led to fast-growing demand for information and analytics across the enterprise. Analysts were already spending too much of their time generating reports rather than building models—and the demand for reports was relentless. The response was to empower and equip the growing number of analytical amateurs by rapidly deploying data warehouses and automating common analyses and report formats. The analyst groups also partnered with Six Sigma and other groups to give analysts more opportunity to work on high-priority and high-value business projects.

Driving to Become an Analytical Enterprise

Best Buy, the *Fortune* 100 consumer electronics retailer, has made analytics a critical component of how it works and competes ever since 1997, when it embarked on a two-year "scientific retailing" initiative that led to a major financial turnaround. In 2004, when former CEO Brad Anderson began to emphasize "customer centricity" as a means of maintaining the company's growth trajectory, managers felt that it was time for a review of the role of analytics in the company. By 2006, Anderson and other top executives were convinced that the key to the company's future lay in building an enterprisewide analytical capability. Their motivation was to drive data and decision making to individual stores, where employees are closest to their customers.

At the corporate level, customer segmentation and data warehousing quickly became a priority. Though quality data about customers was available and customer behaviors were documented, they were often not well understood. More importantly, they were not being used systematically to make fact-based decisions, especially at the store level. As Shari Ballard, Best Buy's executive vice president of channels, explains:

> We needed to make sure that the district, territory, and store teams have the tools that they need to actually look at things like: what kind of traffic do they have coming in their stores today, how effectively are they selling to the people that are in the stores today, what do their close rates look like, what does their customer sat[isfaction] information look like, what segments do they have coming in, what kind of market share do they have for those segments? We have invested in the right tools so that the field knows what to focus and can identify what indicators to move a little bit that will help us a lot."[4]

So Best Buy assembled a team of business and technology professionals to launch an initiative that would redefine how the company deploys, uses, and integrates analytics for better decision making and business outcomes. The project leader was Marc Gordon, vice president of Financial Planning and Analysis—an area with both the analytical capability and the visibility needed to make the project effective.

The team's goals were encapsulated in what became an organizational mantra: "Think differently, act differently, drive different outcomes." The team started by identifying and defining the metrics to build an enterprise performance management capability—basically a framework for organizing and analyzing business processes, metrics, and systems to identify ways to optimize performance. Ultimately, the capability would give stores and functional groups access to actionable insights about their customers for the first time and enable them to integrate fact-based decisions into their daily business routines. It would also create a new, enterprisewide culture of analytics, disseminating and revitalizing the headquarters' analytical focus.

The team's next challenge was to work with representatives from each functional area to define metrics. Eschewing conventional approaches, the team defined metrics in a way that best reflected Best Buy's commitment to customer centricity, using three key fact-based questions: What happened? Why did it happen? What *should* happen?

Armed with an understanding of the most valuable metrics, the team has started to embed them in a closed-loop process (see figure 10-2) that would build and test new analytical capabilities and integrate them throughout the organization. Best Buy recognizes that this process will take some time to mature.

FIGURE 10-2

Best Buy's closed-loop analytics model

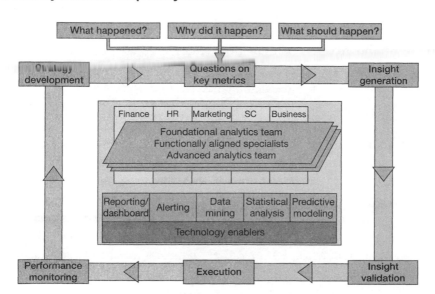

Though functional groups had been collecting and reporting data for some time, analytics were not trusted enterprisewide, and employees were hesitant to embrace a new lexicon for metrics, let alone use new analytical ways to make business decisions. The challenge of reaching an accord often prolonged the integration process but ultimately encouraged the introduction of an analytical culture across functional areas and in the stores.

To spur on analytical success, the team deployed an innovative scorecard and reporting tool to give business operators across the organization access to new data and customer insights that would fuel analytical decisions. They also established a training program to teach the sales force how to identify and serve different types of customers and how to interpret and act on the daily data they began to receive.

The analytical organization was the next focus. Realizing that store managers would require help with advanced or specialized analysis, the team created the Reporting and Analytics Support Capability (RASC), a centralized group responsible for maintaining the consistency of Best Buy's analytical capability by providing critical information about performance to business operators from the store level to the corporate level. It also gave store managers someone to call at corporate headquarters to help them analyze and influence customer behavior.

For example, the RASC group worked with one district to help them grow market penetration among older Americans, especially empty nesters. They found that most empty nester purchases were items like appliances or DVDs that did not require technology knowledge. RASC analyzed the reasons behind lower than predicted technology purchases and assessed possible actions to increase sales. Based on these insights, the district general manager teamed with AARP to provide technology education classes at the local library, resulting in a significant increase in technology sales among empty nesters.

At about the same time, Best Buy created central organizational groups within functional areas for marketing, supply chain, and human resource analytics. As operations across the enterprise embraced their new analytical capabilities, success stories began to emerge. Store managers began to use data-driven insights to review business practices and to seize new opportunities. On one earnings call, Shari Ballard called attention to two specific general managers who had used analytics to develop initiatives for underserved customers in their areas. These positive acknowledgments from the top further reinforced the value of fact-based decision making.

Feedback from the stores to the executive suite has been extremely positive. Best Buy continues to embrace analytical capabilities and talent as crucial to its business. And former CEO Brad Anderson sees customer-focused analytics as a bright spot in an otherwise challenging market: "While we see the [economic] climate as serious and very difficult, we have an enormous amount of confidence in the skills and talent of the people we've got and the approach of finding customer-centric value propositions to influence our results."[5]

Best Buy is committed to becoming a more and more analytical enterprise. You can see from their story that a lot depends on leadership and on rallying around an analytically enabled business focus of paramount importance. You see the company building all five of the DELTA elements—data, enterprise, leadership, targets, and analysts. You also see executives taking the actions we describe in part 2—reviewing their business methods and use of analytics, embedding analytics into both performance management and store-level decision making, and fostering an analytical culture across the enterprise. If your organization decides to take analytics to the next level and become a thoroughly analytical enterprise, your road may be quite different from Best Buy's. But your success factors, and the signposts and challenges along the road, will be similar.

11

Toward More Analytical
Decisions and Better Results

LIFE WOULD BE A lot simpler if everything we've suggested up till now could be accomplished by executive fiat. But like anything worthwhile, putting analytics to work takes effort and thought. In this book, we've described the elements an organization needs to establish a sustainable, robust, enterprisewide analytical capability.

We want to share a final piece of advice: begin with the end in mind. We hear the devoted users of analytics say, "All the analytics in the world won't help unless we *use them* to make and execute better decisions," and we expect other firms will realize this as they become more proficient in the use of analytics.

Toward Fact-Based Decisions

Analytics at Work, then, is all about making (and acting on) better decisions based on facts and analysis. This may not seem like a new idea; after all, better information systems and data were always intended to facilitate better decisions, but for the first fifty years of the information age, they mostly facilitated information transactions and the capture of data. Now that organizations are beginning to master analytics, they can better address how decisions are made and executed, how they can be improved, and how information is used to support them. And they must look at all types of decisions: from strategic planning decisions

175

made by senior management to everyday operational decisions, whether made by employees on the front line or automated by back-end systems. Over the long term, companies should attend to decisions directly—and not assume that better information and analytical tools will automatically lead to better decisions.

What are *fact-based decisions*? We propose the following definition:

> Fact-based decisions employ objective data and analysis as the primary guides to decision making. The goal of these guides is to get at the most objective answer through a rational and fair-minded process, one that is not colored by conventional wisdom or personal biases. Whenever feasible, fact-based decision makers rely on the scientific method—with hypotheses and testing—and rigorous quantitative analysis. They eschew deliberations that are primarily based on intuition, gut feeling, hearsay, or faith, although each of these may be helpful in framing or assessing a fact-based decision.

Note that our definition specifies that data and analysis are supposed to be used to discover the *most objective answers*. Yes, we know that statistics and figures can be manipulated to support dishonestly whatever point someone wants to demonstrate; despite the old adage, the numbers do lie, just like the people who manufacture them.[1] But assuming your intentions are honorable, you will probably find the most objective answer more readily with data and rigorous analysis than with any other method. The definition also acknowledges that facts aren't the only way to discover the best possible answer. While the attribute "fact-based" seems synonymous with "virtuous," at least in contemporary business, there is some leeway for intuition and experience in decision making.

Managing Decisions as a Process

Decision making is a complex subject—and it's getting more complex all the time. Most organizations haven't focused on improving decisions because they have long been considered the prerogative of individuals—usually senior executives—and such decisions have been something of a "black box." Information goes in, decisions come out, and it's hard to know what happens in between. Fortunately, focusing on decisions doesn't rely solely on insight into the mental processes of managers, but also on the outward manifestations of decisions—what decisions need to be made, what information is supplied, the key roles in the decision process, how accurate or effective the decisions turn out to be, and so forth.

If you are going to manage decisions, you should design and manage them as seriously as you do your business processes. As with any other process, streamlining a decision process will save time, cut cost, improve quality, and yield better results. And because many critical decisions with far-reaching implications (like pricing strategies) cross functional boundaries, it is important to make sure that they work well across the entire organization.

For example, an organization that focuses heavily on decisions and how data and analysis can be applied to them would make a list of key decisions—"key" being whatever criteria the organization cares about. It could be the "top ten decisions required to execute our strategy" or "the top twenty decisions that have to go well for us to meet our financial goals." Without some inventory and prioritization, all decisions will be treated as equals, and most likely won't be addressed at all. In a sense, these are the decision "targets" to which analytics and other improvement approaches can be applied, and they should be consistent with the business targets for analytics as discussed in chapter 5.

In addition to creating an inventory of decisions, these organizations would classify major decisions by their attributes. Who plays what role in the decision, or what is its governance? How frequently does it recur? How structured is it? What information is available to support it? By classifying, an organization can begin to determine which interventions might make the decision more effective and to establish a common language for discussing a decision within the organization.[2]

A decision-focused organization would also have approaches to review and continuously improve its decision-making processes, such as a Six Sigma–style function or a Tiger team whose members come from the business processes that are affected by the decision. Moreover, a decision-focused organization would have a group of decision "engineers," coaches, or consultants for improving decisions. At GE Capital, for example, a group of about four hundred analysts reside within a "decision management" organization. Instead of just supplying analytics and correct answers, the goal of the analysts is to work with executives to improve decision processes.

Organizations that care about decisions would assess their managers and employees based on the decisions they've made. Assessing results can get political quickly, but assessing the process and information used for key decisions can be very constructive. A few organizations, including Swiss engineering giant ABB, already do this for some managers. They make this assessment an established part of the performance review process.

Another key attribute to improving decisions is "metadecision analysis." This simply means that before making a decision, a person or organization should ask, "How should we make this decision?" While the question may seem obvious, it is rarely asked in an explicit and methodical way.

At Air Products, a five-step process is recommended for making important decisions. Step 1 is to define the decision to be made. Steps 2 and 3 might be considered metadecision analysis; they are to "determine method" and "establish governance." The method to be adopted involves the level of participation—whether a decision is determined unilaterally, consultatively, by a majority, or by consensus. Governance follows the well-established RACI approach in project management: who is expected to be responsible, accountable, consulted, or informed?[3] Step 4 is to make the decision; step 5 is to communicate and implement it. All five steps are perhaps not necessary for deciding what to have for lunch, but you'd probably end up with a satisfying meal.

Why is such a metadecision approach important? It's because there are many different ways to make decisions today, but they all require stepping back and thinking about the decision process and the best ways to accomplish it. Air Products' approach is far better than what most organizations do, but there are many more possibilities and options to choose from.

These approaches are just beginning to be addressed by analytically focused organizations. Some have concluded that organizing for analytics is less valuable than organizing for "decision management." In financial services firms, in particular, decision management groups have been created to centralize decision-oriented assistance across product lines. In addition to GE Capital, Royal Bank of Scotland and Citi have also formed such organizations. They have not been involved in all recent decisions (including, fortunately, the subprime mortgage investments at each bank), but they are beginning to lend "decision support"—sometimes based on analytics, sometimes based on other approaches—to key decisions across the organization.

Even in the tough times for financial services firms that we've been going through, GE Capital has made a lot of money for GE ($9 billion in 2008 profits). Analytically focused executives in the GE Money consumer finance unit of GE Capital concluded that just having analysts come up with the right answer wasn't enough for the company. They decided to move from an analytics group to a decision management group because the ultimate end is for people or systems to make the right decision. It has to be made at the right time and in the right context, and any analyses either have to be embedded in sound business processes, or have to be well understood by human decision makers to ensure that the decision is made the right way. GE Money's group has worked on analytics-heavy decisions involving marketing, risk management, loan underwriting, and even human resources. The decision management group has worked out well enough that GE Capital has decided to adopt it across the entire organization.

Today only a few other companies have groups like GE's, but we expect that decision management will grow in importance over time, and that more organizations will establish such groups. Even if you're not ready to go that far, you can begin to focus on fact-based decision making in your own group or department. Take a single decision that's important to your organization and do a bit of meta-analysis on it. What actions will arise from the decision? How does the decision contribute to business performance? Who is playing the various decision roles? What information will be used to make the decision, and what's the desired linkage to the decision process? What are some ways in which the decision process might be improved? If you are really adventurous, you might even try to determine how the quality of the decision might be assessed and tracked over time. None of these approaches is terribly difficult. We think that adopting them—and then executing those decisions consistently, efficiently, and at scale—is the next frontier for analytically oriented organizations, which is why we've concluded with the topic.

What We Promise and What We Don't

We're confident you'll get a lot of value from the nostrums in this book; otherwise, we wouldn't have written it. But we also want to specify what we do promise to organizations that adopt these ideas, and what we don't—a sort of "truth in writing." Consistent with this chapter's focus, most of the statements below involve the extent to which analytics will actually improve decisions. First, let's get the cautionary messages out of the way:

Analytical Decisions Aren't the Only Ones That Will Lead to Success. Unlike some business book authors, we know there are multiple routes to success within any industry. As Harrah's CEO Gary Loveman noted in the foreword to *Competing on Analytics*, his competitor Steve Wynn isn't noted for his orientation to analytical methods. Yet his intuitive sense of luxury and style has led his company, Wynn Resorts, to prosper (at least up until the current financial crisis). In every industry, executives with experience, intuition, and luck may choose strategies that pay off without benefit of data and analysis. But it's clear that in almost every industry you'll have a successful analytical competitor, and unless you are awfully confident in your experience, intuition, and luck, you should be using facts to improve your decisions.

Your Analytical Decisions Won't Always Be Perfect. In most cases, gathering and analyzing data significantly increases the likelihood that your answer will be right, or at least better than a guess. One pharmaceutical CEO mused to us that if analytics could boost his company's drug-picking ability from, say, 10 percent to 40 percent, he'd see a huge improvement to the bottom line—even though he'd still be off most of the time. Sometimes, your analytical decision will be wrong or suboptimal. Analytics may lead you to charge a price that's less than the customer would pay. Analytics may predict that a patient shouldn't contract a disease, but he or she will get it anyway. Analytics may lead you to choose a player for your sports team who should be great, but who bombs. Indeed, one of the biggest hurdles organizations face is learning (through review) not to keep making the same bet when the model was wrong the last time. But don't lose faith in data and analytics. You're better off overall making analytical decisions, even if sometimes you end up on the wrong side of a statistical distribution of outcomes.

You'll Need to Develop New Analytically Based Insights to Stay Ahead of the Competition. Analytical companies are like sharks, continually on the prowl for the next insight. Why? Eventually your competitors will catch on and duplicate your innovations. This happens faster in industries where there is more transparency and sharper competition. But sooner or later competitors will get on the analytics bandwagon and start to build their own analytical models. Resting on your laurels is simply not an option.

Sometimes the World Will Change, and Invalidate the Models That Guide Your Decisions. As we discussed in chapter 9, the world turns and makes your data and analyses no longer relevant. If you choose to live by analytics, you are also choosing to constantly evaluate and change them. Make your hypotheses and assumptions clear, and be attuned to when they might need changing. As a final example, take price optimization for retail stores. We're big fans of this analytical application because most of its adopters say that it has improved profit margins dramatically. But as we write, with the economy in free fall, retailers may want to update their historical models of price elasticity in deciding what to put on sale when. Part of benefiting from history is knowing when history doesn't apply.[4]

Analytics Are Not All You Need to Make Good Decisions. Use all the tools at your disposal to make better decisions. In addition to data and analytics, those tools include experience, intuition, group process, and even taking votes or structuring predictive opinion markets. Sometimes the results will conflict with each other, or perhaps analytical results will contradict your own wisdom. You don't want to ignore the contradictions; use them to justify a closer look at the data and the analysis and examine the implicit assumptions of your experience.

Okay, now we've done our fiduciary duty. On the positive side, we promise:

You'll Make Better Strategic Decisions. Strategic decisions are occasional, important decisions that can benefit from systematic analysis and data gathering. If you're trying to decide whether to buy or merge with another company, enter a new market, introduce a new product, or go after a different type of customer, you'll benefit from analytical decision making. Granted, you'll still need some good intuition, but analytics will certainly provide a clearer sense of what you're trying to accomplish since they will show you how intangibles impact things like growth and profitability.

You'll Make Better Tactical and Operational Decisions. These are the meat and potatoes of analytics because they're decisions that recur frequently and are based on operations that create lots of data. If you systematically collect and analyze the data, you can improve how you produce, price, market, and sell your product or service. Recurring decisions are worthy of your investment in better, more analytical decision processes. If you make a few more euros (or yen or dollars or bolivars) on each of these transactions because of analytics, the total benefit over time will be dramatic.

You'll Have a Better Ability to Solve Problems. Data and analytics often provide the key to why something is happening in your organization. If something is going wrong, gathering and analyzing data on the circumstances in which the problem occurs is one of the best ways to get to its source. Whether your problem involves customers (say, they're not turning out in the expected numbers), your supply chain (it has more inventory than you would expect for this time of year), or even employees (the new hiring criteria don't seem to be working out), analytics can help you solve it.

You'll Have Better Business Processes. If, as we advocated in chapter 7, you embed analytics into your core business processes, they will perform better. Processes are a structured way to think about how work gets done, and analytics are a structured way to think about the decisions made within those processes. They make for a great combination. We think that the future of analytics—at least for operational decisions—will be intimately connected with the future of business process thinking, and vice versa.

You'll Be Able to Make Faster Decisions and Get More Consistent Results. Analytics sometimes take a while to create in the first place, but once you have an algorithm or a scoring model, you can scale and run it thousands or even millions of times, in only a few seconds. By using the rules and models developed by your best experts, you can ensure that decisions are made correctly and consistently across the organization.

You'll Be Able to Anticipate Shifting Trends and Market Conditions. Monitoring and close analysis of external market factors can provide an early warning sign of economic and market shifts, help identify new opportunities, and anticipate changing customer tastes. If executed well, analytics can even improve your ability to change your mind about what's driving your business. If you practice good "model management," you'll be able to quickly determine whether your predictive models are still predicting well, and whether your optimizing models are still optimized. You'll be able to see the assumptions behind the models, and to figure out whether they still apply. When they no longer apply, or fail to predict effectively, that's very valuable information, too—what quants call "a canary in a coal mine."

You'll Get Better Business Results. In our previous book on analytics we found (in two separate studies) that firms that made more use of analytics tended to perform better financially. We continue to observe that analytical companies generally lead their industries in performance. Analytical conservatism forces us to point out that this may not be a causal relationship, but we believe it is. It's easy to see—and we've provided many examples in this book—how investments in analytics could yield both more revenue on the top line and more profit on the bottom line. Of course, some applications will yield more direct financial benefits than others. We have generally found, for example, that pricing applications provide the most direct link between analytics and more money. And if your organization's mission involves something other than making money, you can probably do it better with analytics too.

Our view—and we see confirmation of it almost everywhere we look—is that data and analytics are steadily becoming more important and influential in every organization. More data becomes available every day. More powerful software and hardware are constantly emerging to help analyze and interpret the data. More people are spilling out of universities with the ability to analyze data and make analytical decisions. As Larry Summers, former treasury secretary and president of Harvard University, and now chief economic adviser to the Obama administration, put it: "I suspect that when the history is written two hundred years from now, [a trend] will emerge as something very important that happened in human thinking during the time when we were alive, and that is that we are becoming rational, analytical, and data-driven in a far wider range of activity than we ever have been before."[5] Summers isn't always right, but we're pretty confident he's right in this case.

Analytics and fact-based decisions are a trend for the ages. Other decision approaches will rise and fall, but the progress toward fact-based techniques will be inexorable. It's time for every organization to address both how to make better decisions today, and how to sustain high performance across business cycles and generations.

Appendix

The DELTA Transitions

In chapters 2–6 we discussed what the analytical journey looks like for each of the DELTA elements—data, enterprise, leadership, targets, and analysts. Here, for your convenience, we put that information together into a complete picture. In table A-1, we outline what conditions are typically in place at each stage of progress in deploying analytical business applications with impact. Its two dimensions are the DELTA success factors and the five-stage journey to being an analytical competitor. The combination is a kind of map, a high-level assessment tool for analytical capability. Take a few minutes to study it, and notice how the DELTA elements align with any given stage, and how each element evolves across the stages.

Companies have found this mapping handy for a variety of tasks:

- Assessing where you are—what are your analytical capabilities, strengths, and weaknesses?

- Recognizing where to go next—what strengths can you capitalize on, and what gaps should you try to close?

- Setting reasonable ambitions—what can you hope to accomplish and when?

- Monitoring progress—how fast and how far are you traveling on the journey to capitalize on analytics?

- Perhaps most important, discussing all these things with executive leadership and everyone else with an interest in succeeding with analytics—how can you come to mutual understanding about your capabilities and commitment to a plan of action?

The DELTA transitions

	From Stage 1 *Analytically Impaired* to Stage 2 *Localized Analytics*	From Stage 2 *Localized Analytics* to Stage 3 *Analytical Aspirations*	From Stage 3 *Analytical Aspirations* to Stage 4 *Analytical Companies*	From Stage 4 *Analytical Companies* to Stage 5 *Analytical Competitors*
Data	Gain mastery over local data of importance, including building functional data marts.	Build enterprise consensus around some analytical targets and their data needs. Build some domain data warehouses (e.g., customer) and corresponding analytical expertise. Motivate and reward cross-functional data contributions and management.	Build enterprise data warehouses and integrate external data. Engage senior executives in EDW plans and management. Monitor emerging data sources.	Educate and engage senior executives in competitive potential of analytical data. Exploit unique data. Establish strong data governance, especially stewardship. Form a BICC if you don't have one yet.
Enterprise	Find allies for small-scale analytics projects that nonetheless suggest cross-functional or enterprise potential. Manage data risk at local level. Partner with IT on common tool selection and data standards.	Select applications with relevance to multiple business areas. Keep scope manageable, but with an eye to future expansion. Establish standards for data privacy and security. Begin building enterprise analytical infrastructure incrementally.	Develop analytics strategy and road map for major business unit, if not the enterprise. Conduct risk assessments of all analytical applications. Establish enterprise governance of technology and architecture for analytics.	Manage analytical priorities and assets at the enterprise level. Implement enterprisewide model review and management. Extend analytics tools and infrastructure broadly and deeply across the enterprise.
Leadership	Encourage the emergence of analytical leaders in functions and business units.	Create a vision of how analytics will be used in the organization in the future, and begin to identify the specific capabilities necessary.	Engage senior leaders in building analytical capabilities, particularly in the areas of data, technology, and analytical human resources.	Encourage leaders to be visible with their analytical capabilities, and to communicate with internal and external stakeholders about how analytics contribute to success.

Targets	Work wherever there is sponsorship and some decent data. Target "low-hanging fruit."	Work with business areas that are already somewhat analytical or can benefit greatly from analytics. Target business process or cross-functional applications. Start taking systematic inventories of analytical opportunities by business area.	Work with major business processes and their owners. Focus on high value and high impact targets. Take an enterprisewide approach to finding and evaluating targets. Formalize the process of targeting as a collaboration among business executives, IT and analytics leaders.	Work with the executive team. Focus on strategic initiatives, value creation, and building distinctive capability that will enhance competitive differentiation. Infiltrate the strategic planning process so analytics can shape (not just respond to) business strategy.
Analysts	Identify pockets of analysts and skills. Offer analytical skills training. Encourage analytical components of systems projects. Enlist managers to appreciate and engage analytical employees.	Define analytical positions and use specialty recruiting sources to fill them. Encourage knowledge sharing among analysts of all types. Promote rotational deployment of analysts. Provide coaching and support, especially for analytical professionals.	Evaluate analytical expertise of all information workers, develop relationships with universities and associations, and provide advanced training for analysts. Focus on developing business acumen in analysts and analytical expertise in business executives. Integrate the development and deployment process. Form communities of analysts.	Hire analytically minded employees in all business roles. Formalize an analyst-role/business-role rotation program. Organize and deploy analysts centrally. Regularly recognize analytical employees in all roles, and ensure that analysts are constantly challenged in their work.

Study this table with your current condition and analytical ambitions in mind. What do you need to do to leverage your strengths, shore up your weaknesses, become more DELTA ready, and increase the business impact and value of analytics? As you consider your course of action, be sure to avoid the most common pitfalls:

- Focusing too much on one dimension of analytical capability (most often technology and data) at the expense of the others.

- Devoting too much time, energy, and money on analytical initiatives that have low business impact (even if that's what the business is asking for).

- Attempting to do too much at once.

Notes

Chapter 1

1. Accenture survey of 254 U.S. managers; see "Most U.S. Companies Say Business Analytics Still Future Goal, Not Present Reality," Accenture press release, Dec. 11, 2008, http://newsroom.accenture. com/article_display.cfm?article_id=4777.

2. John W. Tukey, *Exploratory Data Analysis* (Reading, MA: Addison Wesley, 1977); Edward Tufte, *The Visual Display of Quantitative Information*, 2nd ed. (Cheshire, CT: Graphics Press, 2001).

3. Gary Klein, *Sources of Power: How People Make Decisions* (Cambridge, MA: MIT Press, 1999).

4. Interview with Mike Linton, February 15, 2006.

5. Nassim Nicholas Taleb, *The Black Swan: The Impact of the Highly Improbable* (New York: Random House, 2007)

6. Cameron French, "TransAlta Says Clerical Snafu Costs It $24 Million," GlobeandMail.com, June 3, 2003, http://www.globeinvestor.com/servlet/ArticleNews/story/ROC/20030603/2003-06-03T232028Z_01_N03354432_RTRIDST_0_BUSINESS-ENERGY-TRANSALTA-COL.

7. Jonathan B. Cox, "Incentive Model Called Too Rosy," *Raleigh (NC) News and Observer*, March 22, 2007, http://www2.nccommerce.com/eclipsfiles/16386.pdf.

8. Carol Hymowitz, "Companies Need CEOs to Stop Spinning and Start Thinking," *Wall Street Journal*, December 19, 2007.

9. David Olive, "Getting Wise Before That 'One Big Mistake,'" *Toronto Star*, December 17, 2007, B1.

10. Willy Shih, Stephen Kaufman, and David Spinola, "Netflix," Case 9-607-138 (Boston: Harvard Business School, revised November 19, 2007).

Chapter 2

1. Interview with Al Parisian, January 2009, and e-mail correspondence.

2. Chuck Salter, "Why America Is Addicted to Olive Garden," *Fast Company*, July 1, 2009, http://www.fastcompany.com/magazine/137/why-america-is-addicted-to-olive-garden.html.

3. Mark McClusky, "The Nike Experiment: How the Shoe Giant Unleashed the Power of Personal Metrics," *Wired*, June 22, 2009, http://www.wired.com/medtech/health/magazine/17-07/lbnp_nike.

4. Accenture, "Helping the Royal Shakespeare Company Achieve High Performance Through Audience Analytics, Segmentation and Targeted Marketing," 2008, http://www.accenture.com/NR/rdonlyres/891F5AA1- A1C2-4828-81E8-BE4EBAD7948B/0/RSCcredentialFinal.pdf.

5. Mary Hayes Weier, "Coke's Customer-Loyalty Web Site Scores Big with Consumers," *Information Week*, July 21, 2008.

6. In the business intelligence (BI) world, this is known as the "Field of Dreams" approach. But if you build it, they will not come—and anyway, you will probably suffer in the effort.

7. Blog post by Judah Phillips of Web Analytics Demystified, July 19, 2008, http://judah.webanalyticsdemystified.com/2007/08/web-analytics-data-quality.html.

8. From an enterprise IT perspective, a data mart and an EDW serve different purposes. An EDW is truly a warehouse—a storage area where you can get bulk deliveries of very detailed data to fill the "store shelves." A mart is more like a grocery store, where items are already sitting on store shelves, packaged and ready for consumption.

9. "Getting a Handle on Our Information! Information Stewardship at BMO FG" (document furnished to author), May 12, 2006, and discussion with BMO executives, April 19, 2007. This document suggests that BICCs are responsible for two key data functions: acquisition and stewardship. Acquisition includes activities such as data integration, data storage, testing, and maintenance. Stewardship includes the responsibility for data standards, quality, and governance.

10. Gloria J. Miller, Dagmar Brautigam, and Stefanie V. Gerlach, *Business Intelligence Competency Centers: A Team Approach to Maximizing Competitive Advantage* (New York: John Wiley & Sons, 2006), 38.

11. Interview with Lisa Tourville, March 6, 2008.

12. Interview with David Donkin, October 28, 2006; Wayne Eckerson, "New Ways to Organize the BI Team," Data Warehousing Institute *Business Intelligence Journal*, March 28, 2006, http://www.tdwi.org/Publications/BIJournal/display.aspx?ID=7896.

Chapter 3

1. Interview with Robin deHaan and Venkat Parakala, February 7, 2009.

2. Accenture Information Management Services survey of more than 250 executives is the basis of a report, "Competing Through Business Analytics," which studied companies' use of and investment in analytics to remain competitive. December, 2008.

3. Jeanne G. Harris and Thomas Davenport, "New Growth from Enterprise Systems: Achieving High Performance Through Distinctive Capabilities," Research report, Accenture Institute for High Performance, 2006, 10.

4. Interview with Jim Kolsky and Mike Van Houten, July 17, 2008.

5. For a discussion of the enterprise IT architecture needed for business intelligence and analytics, see Thomas H. Davenport and Jeanne G. Harris, *Competing on Analytics* (Boston: Harvard Business School Press, 2007), chapter 8, "The Architecture of Business Intelligence."

6. David L. Hill and Jeanne G. Harris, "Using Enterprise Systems to Gain Uncommon Competitive Advantage," *Outlook* 1 (2007): 65–71.

7. Andrew K. Reese, "Planning to Succeed at Procter & Gamble," *Supply & Demand Chain Executive* 8, no. 2 (February 1, 2007): 20.

8. Interview with Pradeep Kumar, June 24, 2009.

Chapter 4

1. Thomas H. Davenport, Jeanne G. Harris, David DeLong, and Al Jacobsen, "Data to Knowledge to Results: Building an Analytic Capability," *California Management Review* 43/2 (Winter 2001): 117–138.

Chapter 5

1. Interview with Shannon Baillet-Antorcha, January 20, 2009.

2. Thomas H. Davenport and Jeanne G. Harris, *Competing on Analytics* (Boston: Harvard Business School Press, 2007), 9.

3. Leahy quote from George Anderson, "Part I: Tesco's Leahy ID's Global Opportunities," Retail Wire Discussions series, http://www.retail wire.com/Discussions/Sngl_Discussion.cfm/12090.

4. For a useful framework describing three different business types and how they create value, see Øystein D. Fjeldstad and Espen Andersen, "Casting Off the Chains: Value Shops and Value Networks," *European Business Forum* 14 (Summer 2003): 47–53. See also Charles B. Stabell and Øystein D. Fjeldstad, "Configuring Value for Competitive Advantage: On Chains, Shops, and Networks," *Strategic Management Journal* 19 (1998): 413–437.

Chapter 6

1. Jeanne G. Harris, Elizabeth Craig, and Henry Egan, "How to Create the Talent-Powered Analytical Organization" research report, Accenture Institute for High Performance, 2009.

2. Interview with Dr. Steven Udvarhelyi, December 10, 2008.

3. Interview with Kyle Cheek, November 24, 2008. Kyle Cheek has moved to another company since we interviewed him for this book and is now vice president of data services and analytics at Emdeon Business Services.

4. Interview with Daryl Wansink, January 29, 2009.

5. Interview with David Scamehorn, December 31, 2008. Scamehorn has moved to another company since we interviewed him for this book and is now director of customer analytics at Advance Auto Parts.

6. "Will Smith Voted 2008's Top Money-Making Movie Star," www. reuters.com/article/entertainmentNews/idUSTRE5013DY20090102, Reuters newswire, January 2, 2009.

7. R. Grover, "Box Office Brawn," *BusinessWeek*, January 14, 2008, 18.

8. Scott Bowles, "Will Smith Has Found the Magic Formula," *USA Today*, June 26, 2008.

9. R.W. Keegan, "The Legend of Will Smith," *Time*, November 29, 2007.

10. Christopher Kelly, "Box-office champ Smith says 'Seven Pounds' offers him the chance to shed old persona" December 16, 2008, http://www.popmatters.com/pm/article/67010-box-office-champ-smith-says-seven-pounds-offers-him-the-chance-to-she/ or this one from the Will Smith fan site, http://www.willsmithweb.com/2008/12/14/seven-pounds%e2%80%99-offers-chance-to-shed-some-of-his-old-persona/.

11. Interview with Byrne Doyle, January 6, 2009. Since our interview, Doyle has been promoted to vice president, territory general manager, a significant promotion.

12. A common misconception is that most analytical workers lack broader business know-how. In fact, our research found that analytical workers had higher levels of business acumen than their non-analytical counterparts. Analysts in our study showed a greater and often more nuanced understanding of their company's strategy, goals, and core capabilities, as well as the impact of external forces on their organization—such as the actions of competitors or regulators. Analytical champions scored highest on business acumen, which is needed to align analytical capabilities with business priorities. Professionals had high levels of business acumen as well. It's clear that, despite their deep technical skills, pros are not just backroom statisticians, but also must possess strong business insight.

13. Warren E. Buffett, Annual Letter to Shareholders of Berkshire Hathaway, 2008, http://www.berkshirehathaway.com/letters/2008ltr.pdf.

14. Interview with Sharon Frazee, November 10, 2008.

15. This section adopts a framework published in Peter Cheese, Robert J. Thomas, and Elizabeth Craig, *The Talent Powered Organization* (London: Kogan Page, 2007).

16. Jeanne G. Harris, Elizabeth Craig, and Henry Egan, "How to Organize Your Analytical Talent," research report, Accenture Institute for High Performance, 2009.

17. These Web sites include quantfinancejobs.com, jobs.phd.org, wilmott.com, and quantster.com.

18. Internal Accenture analysis, 2009.

19. On September 21, 2009, Netflix declared "BellKor's Pragmatic Chaos," a global group of researchers, scientists, and engineers, as winners of its $1 million contest to improve Cinematch. The winning entry improved the model's performance by 10.6 percent.

20. *Good Will Hunting*, Miramax, 1997.

21. Interview with Cathy Mildenhall, May 25, 2007, and March 10, 2008.

Part Two

1. Gary Loveman, foreword, in Thomas H. Davenport and Jeanne G. Harris, *Competing on Analytics* (Boston: Harvard Business School Press, 2007), x.

Chapter 7

1. "Optimization Drives $19 Million at Avis," www.fico.com/en/FIResourcesLibrary/Avis_Success_2540CS.pdf.

2. Also see Thomas H. Davenport and Jeanne G. Harris, *Competing on Analytics* (Boston: Harvard Business School Press, 2007), 150–152.

Chapter 8

1. Discussion by Teruyuki Minoura, then Toyota's managing director of global purchasing, at 2003 Automotive Parts System Solution Fair held in Tokyo, June 18, 2003, http://www.toyotageorgetown.com/tps.asp.

2. Interview with John D'Amore, May 18, 2009, and e-mail correspondence.

3. Michael Roberto, *Why Great Leaders Don't Take Yes for an Answer* (Upper Saddle River, NJ: Pearson Education/Wharton School Publishing, 2005).

4. Warren Bennis, Daniel Goleman, and Patricia Ward Biederman, *Transparency: Creating a Culture of Candor* (San Francisco: Jossey-Bass, 2008), 3–4.

5. "Profile: Barry Beracha," *St. Louis Commerce Magazine*, November 1999, http://www.stlcommercemagazine.com/archives/november1999/profile.html.

6. The online marketing consultant Jim Novo makes a similar point in his blog. See Jim Novo, "Marketing Productivity Blog," http://blog.jimnovo.com/about-the-blog/

Chapter 9

1. Mathew Maier, "Finding Riches in a Mine of Credit Data," *Business 2.0*, October 1, 2005, http://money.cnn.com/magazines/business2/business2_archive/2005/10/01/8359235/index.htm.

2. "Conning & Co. Study Says Auto Insurers Are Paying Closer Attention to Credit Scores," *Insurance Journal*, August 2, 2001, http://www.insurancejournal.com/news/national/2001/08/02/14177.htm.

3. Interview with Dave Williams, January 29, 2008, and e-mail correspondence.

4. Brian P. Sullivan, "Pricing Sophistication Separates Carriers into Those Who Will Thrive, and Those Who Will Not," *Auto Insurance Report*, May 31, 2004, www.insurquote.com/AIR05-31-04.pdf.

5. The American Airlines yield management story is described in detail in Robert L. Phillips, *Pricing and Revenue Optimization* (Palo Alto, CA: Stanford University Press, 2005), chapter 6.

6. Michael Lewis, *Moneyball: The Art of Winning an Unfair Game* (New York: Norton, 2003).

7. Jahn K. Hakes and Raymond D. Sauer, "The *Moneyball* Anomaly and Payroll Efficiency: A Further Investigation," Clemson University working paper, September 2007.

Chapter 10

1. Interview with Jolie Baasch, October 16, 2007.

2. The American Medical Informatics Association defines *informatics* as "the effective organization, analysis, management, and use of information in health care." See http://www.amia.org/informatics/.

3. Interview with Lisa Tourville, March 6, 2008.

4. Best Buy Q1 FY09 Earnings Call, June 16, 2009.

5. Interview with Marc Gordon, August 14, 2006.

Chapter 11

1. See, for example, Darrell Huff, *How to Lie with Statistics*, revised ed. (New York: Norton, 1993).

2. Paul Rogers and Marcia Blenko, "Who Has the D? How Clear Decision Roles Enhance Organizational Performance," *Harvard Business Review*, January 2006.

3. See, for example, the RACI Diagram entry in Wikipedia, http://en.wikipedia.org/wiki/RACI_diagram (accessed November 28, 2008).

4. However, a Nielsen report in 2009 suggests that for most categories of consumer goods sold at retail, historical pricing elasticities still apply. It's good to have and use data!

5. "Remarks of President Lawrence H. Summers," Harvard School of Public Health Leadership Council, Cambridge, Massachusetts, October 21, 2003, http://www.president.harvard.edu/speeches/summers_2003/hsph_deans_council.php.

Index

About the Authors

TOM DAVENPORT is the President's Distinguished Professor in Information Technology and Management at Babson College, and the Research Director of the International Institute for Analytics (www.iianalytics.com).

Tom has written, coauthored, or edited twelve other books, including the bestselling *Competing on Analytics: The New Science of Winning* (with Jeanne Harris). He also authored the first books on business process reengineering and achieving value from enterprise systems, and the bestseller *Working Knowledge* (with Larry Prusak), on knowledge management. He has written more than one hundred articles for such publications as *Harvard Business Review, MIT Sloan Management Review, California Management Review,* the *Financial Times,* and many other publications. Tom has also been a columnist for *CIO, InformationWeek,* and *Darwin* magazines. In 2003 he was named one of the world's "Top 25 Consultants" by *Consulting* magazine, and in 2005 was named one of the world's top three analysts of business and technology by readers of *Optimize* magazine. In 2007 and 2008 he was named one of the one hundred most influential people in the IT industry by Ziff-Davis magazines. His blog at Harvard Business Online is http://discussionleader. hbsp.com/davenport/.

JEANNE G. HARRIS is executive research fellow and a senior executive at Accenture's Institute for High Performance in Chicago. Jeanne leads the Institute's global research agenda in the areas of information, technology, and analytics. In 2009, Jeanne received *Consulting Magazine's* Women Leaders in Consulting award for Lifetime Achievement. She is the coauthor (with Tom Davenport) of *Competing on Analytics: The New*

Science of Winning. During her thirty-three years at Accenture, Jeanne has consulted to a wide variety of organizations in many different industries worldwide. She has led Accenture's business intelligence, analytics, performance management, knowledge management, and data ware-housing consulting practices. She has worked extensively with clients seeking to improve their managerial information, decision-making, an-alytical, and information management capabilities. Jeanne has au-thored numerous book chapters and articles in leading management publications, including *Harvard Business Review, MIT Sloan Management Review, California Management Review,* and *CIO.* Her research has been quoted extensively by the international business press, including the *Wall Street Journal,* the *Financial Times,* and *Nihon Keizai Shimbun.*

ROBERT MORISON is a highly accomplished business researcher, writer, thought leader, speaker, and management consultant. He has been leading breakthrough research at the intersection of business, technol-ogy, and human asset management for more than twenty years, work-ing with over 300 major organizations and writing or editing more than 150 research reports and management guides on topics ranging from workforce management and business innovation to business process reengineering, collaborative business models, and business analytics. He is coauthor of *Workforce Crisis: How to Beat the Coming Shortage of Skills and Talent* (Harvard Business Press, 2006), and three *Harvard Business Review* articles, one of which received a McKinsey Award as best article of 2004. He has recently been a commentator on workforce issues on *Nightly Business Report* on PBS. He has held research and business services management positions with The Concours Group, CSC Index, and General Electric Information Services Company.